Prayer and Meditation for Middle School Kids

Over 100 Practical and Exciting Prayer Exercises for Religious Education Classes and Church Youth Groups

John B. Hesch

PAULIST PRESS
New York/Mahwah

To my teachers and friends,
and to my friend,
The Reverend William H. Carr,
who is teaching me how to be a priest.

Photos used in this book were courtesy of John B. Hesch.

Library of Congress
Catalog Card Number: 85-60416

ISBN: 0-8091-2723-7

Published by Paulist Press
997 Macarthur Boulevard
Mahwah, New Jersey 07430

Printed and bound in the United States of America

Contents

iii

Musical Prayers

Scriptural Prayers

Symbols and Prayer

More Mantras

Praying for Others

Multi-Media Meditations

Be Creative!

Exercises for Experts

Preface:
Love 'Em or Leave 'Em

Some years back, when I was a naive college student, I boldly walked into the parish religious education office and announced my intention to teach the seventh grade religion class. Fools rush in where angels fear to tread.

Many educators will affirm readily that middle school children are the most difficult to teach, to "handle," or to survive, of all the many grade levels. I have seen many a stalwart soul beg for mercy or fume with frustration after just one hour with a class of seventh graders. Having taught middle school religion classes eight years or so, and having experienced there some of the most exhilarating and devastating moments of my life, and still not really knowing very much, I can say this with full conviction: Love 'em or leave 'em.

The key to success and happiness in the worthwhile enterprise of educating middle school kids is simply that you have to love them, and you have to let them know that you love them. If you really do love them, and if you are able to let them know it, they will do anything (almost) for you, and do it with wonderful zest and joy. Kids of that age hunger for a good relationship with an adult; feed that hunger and they will love you back and enrich your life.

If your motivation for teaching middle school religion is anything other than a real love of the kids, you are doomed to frustration. So if you are bargaining with God or pastor, trying to relieve feelings of guilt, or having trouble saying no to catechist recruiters, pick another age level.

This book is designed to be a practical aid for the teacher. It is only a manual for helping middle school kids to practice prayer. The students also need to receive doctrine, and this will come from other sources.

Remember: love 'em or leave 'em!

Introduction

Middle School Kids Are "In-Between" Kids

Go to the book store and try to find some good books about middle school kids. Don't expect to find very much. There are hundreds and thousands of books about elementary school age children; there are just about as many about high school kids or "youths." But middle school kids fall somewhere in between these two categories, and, sadly, they usually fall right through the cracks!

The book store experience reflects the experience of so many middle school kids. They find themselves in a period of life when changes in themselves seem faster than ever before. They know that they are rapidly leaving childhood behind. Yet they clearly are not on a peer level with senior high school students, to whom, in popular parlance, the terms "teenager" and "adolescent" usually apply. They are lost somewhere in between.

Middle school kids are still deeply rooted in childhood. They are leaving behind a period of time in their lives when they "grew together" as persons and learned to have a basic confidence in their ability to learn and perform certain tasks which they were taught.[1] In the lower grades they learned to work and to accomplish "real" things that reached beyond the fantasy life of the playground and prepared them to function in an adult world. Most notably, in our advanced technological society, they learned to read. They also learned to depend upon and feel comfortable in a structured environment; they learned best in an environment where there was clear authority and an atmosphere of friendly and mild coercion. The lower grade years were a time for self-consolidation. The children became comfortable with their bodies and with their place in society. Sigmund Freud called these years the "latency period" because of the notable lack of stormy crises.

Stormy crises are precisely what most middle school kids have to look forward to as they approach the brink of adolescence. For most, the self-confidence, sense of worth, and contentment with life which characterized their earlier years will quickly fade away as they plunge headlong into an adolescent iden-

---

1. See Erik H. Erikson, *Childhood and Society,* 2nd ed., rev. and enl. (New York: W.W. Norton, 1963), Ch. 7, esp. pp. 258–61.

tity crisis.[2] During this stormy time they must experiment in order to find new and adult roles in society. They must deal with new passions, passions stronger than they have ever felt before. They must learn once again whom to trust and distrust, which ideology to embrace and which to reject. They must develop a new sense of autonomy and identity as persons, even as their bodies change so much that they become "new." Eventually, they must leave behind forever the world of their childhood, take on an adult role in society, and decide whether to raise children of their own.

Middle school kids find themselves in between childhood and adolescence. For a time, they teeter back and forth on the brink. They will play with toy trucks or dolls one minute, and seriously discuss getting a job the next. They love to fantasize, especially if they can imagine themselves to be heroes and heroines; yet they do know a lot about the real world and are very attuned to it. They will engage in a serious discussion of life and death, but suddenly break into gales of helpless giggles. They still have much of the innocence and spontaneity of childhood, and yet understand many things as well as adults do. They are very unpredictable, but easily manipulable.

Middle school kids are very complex young people. Their complexity and their "in-betweenness" can be confusing to their teachers and parents, as well as frustrating. But the would-be catechist can take hope in the knowledge that junior high kids are a little confusing to themselves as well! And it is precisely their "in-betweenness," their unceasing swings from very-much-child to almost-adult, and their delight and excitement about it all, which makes teaching them such an exciting and rewarding undertaking.

Middle School Kids Need a Spiritual Life

Anyone who spends much time with middle school kids, whether parent, teacher, scout leader, or coach, knows that they have an endless list of needs. Indeed, one of their greatest joys is telling their parents and others just what their needs are, and how urgent the situation is! But along with braces, the proper brand of running shoe, trips to the movies, and allowances, middle school kids need a solid spiritual life.

Middle school kids need to have a spiritual life with solid foundation, and they need to keep growing spiritually as they mature. Most of them still pray in the same manner that they did when they were much younger. Their prayer almost invariably takes two forms: "talking to God" and reciting memorized prayers. Most do not realize (and so many of their catechists do not realize, either!) that prayer can and should involve much more than this. But in order to develop and deepen their prayer lives, they need help and guidance. They need to be taught about prayer.

---

2. See Erik H. Erikson, *Identity: Youth and Crisis* (New York: W.W. Norton, 1968).

Middle school kids need to develop their prayer lives within a worshiping community. It is vital to their spiritual growth that they be involved in and come to an appreciation of public worship, especially the Eucharist. They need to know about the sacraments, witnessing all sacraments often, and receiving Communion regularly. They even need to receive the sacrament of reconciliation on a regular basis (unfortunately we practically have to make an apology these days when we say that). Teaching middle school kids about sacraments and liturgy is a wonderfully exciting project, and the kids themselves will love it, too. However, this book will not deal with liturgy and sacraments. An entirely separate book would be required to treat so large a subject, and it seems better not to try to treat liturgy and sacraments here at all rather than to do so poorly and inadequately. Nevertheless, let the reader be warned that this is a necessary component of a youngster's spiritual life, and may not be ignored or passed over.

Middle school kids need to develop an inner spiritual life. They need to learn to be very still and quiet, and to create for themselves times of peaceful solitude. This solitude is not loneliness: it is creative and comforting; it is renewing and nourishing; it builds a person up.

Priest-psychologist Henri J.M. Nouwen describes this spiritual solitude and why it is important.[3] Solitude does not mean simply physical withdrawal from the world, although going off by oneself can contribute to solitude. Rather, solitude is an inner sense of quiet and separation; it is independent of a person's environment.

Achieving such a solitude involves learning to listen to oneself. So much emphasis has been placed recently upon interpersonal sensitivity that a person could forget that he must also listen to his own inner voices. Developing this kind of sensitivity is the beginning of the spiritual life. Each person has a vocation, an inner necessity, and it is only through creating some quiet inner space that this necessity can be discovered.

This inner solitude is different from loneliness because it helps us to deepen our fellowship with others. It is the discovery of the self that enables a person truly to love another. The self-confidence and peace which are achieved through a comfortable solitude enable us to avoid clinging desperately to others in some kind of stranglehold.

A sense of solitude also helps us to work in the world. A person without solitude will relate to the world in a knee-jerk way. That is, he will nervously and anxiously react to events in the world, mostly without any reflection or planning. But the person who acts from solitude acts in a thoughtful, purposeful way. And

---

3. *Reaching Out: The Three Movements of the Spiritual Life* (New York: Doubleday, 1975), pp. 13–44.

so there is alertness and attention to life in solitude. Rather than causing a turning away from the world, solitude helps a person respond to its call.

When I began my work with middle school kids, I assumed that the last thing that interested them was peace and quiet. How wrong I was, how woefully wrong! I was pleasantly surprised to find out that kids that age crave precisely the inner peace and solitude which Nouwen describes, and that they are willing to work fairly hard to achieve it. I discovered that they can become fascinated with meditation, and were capable of meditating for thirty minutes at a stretch (that is not a typographical error; it really does say *thirty* minutes)! Obviously their reactions to prayer and meditation will vary considerably, but any normal class of middle school kids can be taught to meditate and will cooperate with a teacher who can point the way to creative solitude.

Middle school kids almost invariably describe prayer as "talking to God." Few of them remember that communication flows in two directions. Few, if any, will observe spontaneously that prayer is also *listening* to God; not surprisingly, the kids are used to doing all the talking! Yet they are thrilled to discover that when they begin to achieve an inner solitude, not only do they hear their own inner voices, they hear God's voice speaking to their hearts! In that experience, they learn that prayer is not only something to be learned and practiced, but it is a gift from God. They come to realize that God is a reality in their lives, and that they have discovered a whole new world to explore.

Prayer for Middle School Kids

When we take into account the in-betweenness which characterizes middle school kids and their need for developing a sense of inner solitude, we can see that their ways of praying must have certain characteristics if they are to be meaningful and helpful. Prayer forms or exercises which are used must be designed to meet the needs of the kids. They must help them to grow in certain specific ways.

Middle school kids are caught up in a fast-paced, noisy, over-stimulating society. Their prayer must help them to cultivate a sense of personal solitude, a solitude which can be creative and energizing, which provides the opportunity for introspection and quiet reflection, and which helps the kids listen to their own inner voices as they struggle to develop a sense of individual identity.

Middle school kids are beginning to question everything and everyone, themselves included. Their prayer must provide free time and space for them to explore themselves, to discover their new emerging strengths and capabilities. Their prayer must help them to experience their own value and cultivate a feeling of self-worth. It must also help them to respect the freedom and integrity of others, affirming the value of freedom to be oneself, to be unique and different.

Middle school kids need to be taught about prayer. This does *not* mean that they need the teacher to stand before them and explain prayer. It *does* mean that they need to be introduced to many prayer forms through actual practice. They need to "try on" many forms of prayer in order to discover which ones "fit." They need the support of praying with one another, and especially the support and guidance of a loving adult who believes deeply in the value of prayer.

Middle school kids experience many negatives in life: the frustration of being in-between, the discovery of the first pimple, strange and embarrassing changes in their bodies, cruel rejection by other children, etc. Their prayer must help them to face the negatives of life and use them creatively as opportunities for learning and growth. Their prayer must be a source of comfort when the real and fancied tragedies of adolescence strike. Their prayer must support their religious upbringing and values as they venture farther and farther out into a world filled with pagan values and immorality.

Middle school kids need prayer. They need spiritual growth. Often they don't know about that, but when someone helps them to discover and build up their relationship with God, they are both delighted and grateful, and their young lives are changed, often in dramatic and lasting ways. If junior high kids had the vocabulary and the capacity for reflection, they would ask along with Jesus' disciples, "Lord, teach us to pray."

How To Get Started

Yes You Can!

Now that you have read through a few pages of theory about psychology and spirituality for middle school kids, you might be thinking (or yelling), "Help! The only way *I* pray is talking to God or saying prayers. I don't know anything about solitude or meditation. I can't teach this stuff!"

My answer is *"Yes you can!"* Helping middle school kids to learn more about prayer and to pray in different ways is not a job that only experts can do. You don't have to be a priest, nun, or brother. You don't have to be a guru in a loincloth. You don't have to be licensed in TA or TM; a little TLC will do just fine.

You have already taken a first step by getting hold of this book on prayer and meditation experiences for middle school kids. It is designed to be a helpful, practical, "how to" manual that any teacher, professional or volunteer, can use. The directions for helping kids to pray are given in a step by step fashion, and all you need to do right now is to keep reading.

You can learn more about prayer and meditation right along with the kids as you teach them. Try to stay just a step (or even a half of a step) ahead of them. Don't try to snow them with expertise that you don't really have; let them know that this is new for you, too, and that you want to learn along with them. Make a deal with your students: enter into an alliance for learning; become allies as you pray together in ways that are new for all of you.

The meditation exercises in this book are divided into categories (e.g., fantasy prayers, scriptural prayers, etc.). Pick out one category and become comfortable with that kind of prayer experience before you move on to another category. You should do at least three or four exercises in a given category with your class before you move on to another one. You might want to proceed through the categories in the order that they are arranged in the book, but this is not necessary. Generally speaking, the exercises at the beginning of a category will be easier to do with the kids than those toward the end of it.

There are a lot of meditation exercises in this book, and you will not be able to do them all, or even most of them, with your class. Pick out the ones that you feel most comfortable leading, and that you think your students will most enjoy. Save the others for another year.

As you prepare your lesson plan for a class meeting, select and practice the meditation exercise that you will be using. Try it out yourself at least once, especially if it involves the use of music, slides, or other materials. Get used to it so that you know it inside out. If you want, find a friendly child and try it out on him or her before the class meets; this will give you some good feedback about how you can expect the exercise to work.

This book contains some step by step directions about helping the kids to learn to pray. Make sure that you read carefully sections like "Capsule Directions for Tuning In" and "Debriefing: The Essential Ending." Refer back to them often as the school year progresses. When you have troubles, consult the last section, "Trouble Shooting."

Finally, make this book work for you. Take your pencil and mark it up. As you do various exercises, write down how they went, what mistakes you made, and how you might do it differently the next time. If you think of new variations to the exercises, write them down and be ready to try them out.

Finding the Time
Most middle school catechists work in one of two types of programs: either in a parochial school or in a once a week "C.C.D. class." Prayer and meditation exercises may be used in either type of program.

For those teachers lucky enough to work in a parochial school, the choice of prayer times will be more flexible. The first possibility to suggest itself is the regular religion class period. The major problem with this time will be that some of the students will not want to participate; there are always one or two in a class group who will not enjoy prayer or meditation. By choosing another time for prayer, the teacher can make participation voluntary, and therefore will find the going easier. Lunch period, free period, or short times before or after school are all possibilities for prayer times. However, care should be taken that the students do not miss out on something they consider important; otherwise, they will not want to pray. Offering prayer as an alternative to recess, for example, would not be wise.

Catechists who see their students only once a week for a sixty or ninety minute class are locked into that time period. Parochial school teachers may also find that the only available prayer time occurs during the regular religion classes. Even in these circumstances, there are choices about timing. The most obvious prayer times during a class period are at the beginning and end of the period. The reasoning usually goes like this: what better time for us to pray than at the beginning or ending of our time together as we learn about our faith!

10

WRONG! WRONG! WRONG! These are the *worst* times for prayer. At the beginning of the class period, the students are scurrying in and getting settled. They will take a few moments to adjust to their new environment. Inevitably, there will be stragglers or latecomers, whose entry, however quiet, would disturb the prayer of others. The end of the class period is an even worse time for prayer. The students are anxious to leave or move on to other things, and they get very restless; they will find it simply impossible to relax and concentrate.

A better choice for prayer time within a set class period is either ten or fifteen minutes into the period or right in the middle. One of my most successful experiences with a weekly seventh grade class which met for a ninety minute period was to use the prayer time as a sort of break in the middle. It was something different to do, and the students found it to be refreshing and restful. It also gave me the opportunity to prepare them for certain meditation exercises with a relevant presentation.

However it is found and whenever it occurs, the prayer time must not be rushed. It is essential that the kids be able to relax with the experience, and this cannot happen if there is even a mere hint that time is running out. Time is precious, but the kids need to know that it is spent lavishly on prayer. That is an important lesson in itself.

Finding the Space

Choosing a good prayer environment is just as important as choosing a good prayer time. There are many good prayer environments, but the worst of all is the standard classroom. The teacher should be willing to go to almost any lengths to remove the students from their school desks for prayer.

I have prayed with junior high kids in a lot of places, but the best of all was a carpeted basement floor in someone's home. The floor is where the students should always sit for prayer. This in itself is an attractive novelty to them. If the floor is not carpeted or is dirty, carpet squares may be put down. The softer and thicker the carpet, the better.

The prayer space should be empty. A plain carpeted floor is better than a cluttered room; it is also better than a tastefully decorated room. The focus should be on the kids and their prayer, and not on decorations. Many of the meditation exercises which I suggest involve using some kind of symbol as an aid or focus; such symbols are always more powerful when they stand alone and don't have to compete with other decorations.

The prayer space should be ample and cozy. The kids need enough room to spread out; they should not be touching each other during the prayer time. Sitting at least two feet apart aids their concentration and enhances their sense of privacy. On the other hand, the space should be small enough that the kids have a feeling of being gathered in a group together. They should be able to see and hear each other easily so that they may share experiences after prayer. In other words, the teacher must attempt to strike a balance between intimacy and privacy.

The prayer space should be separate. The Gospels tell us that Jesus often went off by himself to pray. That is a good example for us to follow. Having a separate space for prayer makes that time more special. The space, no matter how plain or common, can then take on an air of the sacred and holy. After all, "holy" means "set apart." One year when I was teaching in a large rectangular room, I taught the kids at one end and simply moved them to the other end for prayer. It worked very well, and the prayer space remained separate.

Finally, the prayer space should be quiet. Notice that I said *quiet,* but not silent. It is rare to find any room that is truly silent. There are almost always background noises, and kids need to learn to pray in spite of those noises. Even if the teacher could find a totally silent room, it ultimately would not help the kids; they would still need to learn to pray and meditate with noises in the background, since no one lives in an acoustically sealed environment.

Finding the Right Channel: Tuning In

Whenever I want to play my car radio, I have to move the needle up and down the dial just a little bit to tune in the station just right. Whenever I want to pray, I have to tune myself in. Tuning in is an absolutely essential beginning for every prayer and meditation experience in this book. It is the first thing about prayer that you need to teach the kids.

Tuning in involves settling into a quiet solitude so that prayer can take place. It is the most basic form of meditation, and it is essential. The kids need to learn tuning in well and be comfortable with it. Tuning in is the gateway to success in teaching middle school kids about meditation.

Start by having the kids sit on the floor. They may lean slightly against a wall, but that is not necessary (in fact, some experts would discourage it). Their legs should be in a relaxed position: they may be loosely crossed, or the kids may lay one calf over the top of the other one. Some of the kids will want to try the classic lotus position where the legs are very tightly crossed; I find that this is more distracting to them than helpful.

Tell the kids to sit with their backs perfectly straight. The spinal column should be vertical. At this point you'll have to do some demonstrating, because many kids think that "straight back" means "stiffly arched back," and they will arch their backs into intolerably uncomfortable positions. Sit on the floor yourself, sideways with respect to the students, and show them a straight back and then

a stiffly arched back. Explain the difference. Emphasize that even when the back is straight, it should be relaxed.

Have the kids put their hands somewhere in their laps. It is best not to be too specific about this. If they try to pose their hands in a certain position, it will almost surely not be a relaxed one. They should hold nothing in their hands or laps. Make them put pencils, notebooks, papers, etc., in another place, preferably completely outside of the prayer space.

Have them close their eyes and tell them to notice their breathing and try to concentrate on it. Be prepared for the strange noises and subsequent giggles which will shortly follow. Don't get angry and don't be discouraged. You are asking the kids to try something new, and they will be self-conscious and ill at ease for a while. Just quietly continue to encourage them to think about their breathing, and insist that they close their eyes.

When they have quieted down, or after three or four minutes, ask them to open their eyes and look at you. It is time for you to teach them how to breathe. There are basically two ways for a person to expand the chest and let in air: you can lift your shoulders and ribcage, or you can lower your diaphragm. Breathing from the diaphragm is important for tuning in. As the diaphragm lowers, the belly will bulge out a little, but the shoulders will stay in the same place. Demonstrate the two kinds of breathing for the students and ask them to try both.

Now have the students resume their sitting postures and close their eyes. Ask them to concentrate on their breathing, and make sure they "breathe with their bellies." When they giggle, quietly shush them and continue urging them to concentrate and try it. Tell them to breathe in as deeply and slowly as possible, so slowly and quietly that the breathing becomes completely silent. Tell them to notice whether there is any jerkiness in the flow of air and if so, to smooth it out. Tell them not to pause between the inhalations and exhalations, but to establish a smooth, silent, deep, and continuous flow of air.

The kids will need to try this several times, for a couple of minutes at a time. Let them know before each little drill how long it will take, and that you will tell them when to stop: "We're going to try this for two minutes now, and I'll tell you when the time is up. Keep at it until I tell you."

You may suggest to the students that to help them concentrate on the flow of air, they imagine that it has a color, like red or blue. They can try to visualize the flow of this colored air in and out. Tell them that when they become distracted by noise or daydreams, they should simply return their concentration to the flow of air.

By now, the giggles should mostly be over. If there are a couple of "die-hards," it is time to be very firm. Remember, middle school kids learn best in an atmosphere of mild coercion. As you speak to the kids, particularly when their eyes are shut, use a confident, soothing voice, loud enough for all to hear, but just barely.

After a few drills, help the kids deal with noise distractions. Get them quietly breathing, and then invite them to listen very intensely and try to see how many noises they hear. After a moment of quiet, you might name a couple for them (children on the playground outside, the hum of the radiator, the ticking of the clock, etc.). Tell them not to hang on to those noises, but to let them go. Tell them to let the noises pass right through them as light passes through a clear pane of glass. Let them practice.

At this point the kids should be ready for their first "debriefing." After every significant prayer experience, the kids should be debriefed. They have just done something that might be important or exciting for them, and they will want to talk about that. Debrief them by posing open-ended questions such as these:

14

- How did that make you feel?

- What were you thinking about?

- What was your main emotion during that experience?

- Did you learn anything from that?

- Did you learn anything about yourself (or about God) from that?

- Why do you think that was good (or bad, or boring, or frightening, etc.) for you?

- Do you think God spoke to you?

- Do you think you were listening to God?

For more detailed instructions, see the section "Debriefing: The Essential Ending."

Once the kids have tried tuning in and seem able to do it for two or three minutes without interruption, there should be a discussion of the advantages of this type of prayer. Here are some of the advantages of tuning in:

- The required posture combines relaxation and alertness. It helps a person to pay attention to his prayer, but also helps him to rest.

- The continuous deep breathing and concentration actually tranquilizes a person. It can help to dissipate tension and calm nerves. In fact, it is so good for this that it is an excellent way to go to sleep. That's why it is necessary to sit upright while doing it.

- Tuning in helps people be able to listen to themselves, to hear their own inner voices, to "get into themselves," to become self-aware. It can help people get in touch with their own inner powers, powers far stronger than they ever imagined. Tuning in is empowering.

- Tuning in is also powerful. It can help people focus all of their energy on a particular feeling, or problem, or idea. It helps them to consolidate their various strengths and bring them to bear where they are needed most.

- Tuning in helps a person to be still and quiet enough to hear God speak. Remember, prayer involves having a relationship with God, and while prayer is indeed "talking to God," it is also listening to him.

Capsule Directions for Tuning In

- Sit on the floor with legs in a relaxed and comfortable position.

- Keep back straight but not rigid, so that the spinal column is vertical.

- Place hands on lap. Close eyes.

- Breathe from the diaphragm in smooth, steady, deep, slow, and silent rhythm. Concentrate on the flow of air.

- Let noises pass through as light passes through a clear pane of glass. When distracted, simply return concentration to the flow of air.

- When the meditation time is over, debrief.

First Tries

Here are some simple meditation exercises to try with the kids in the beginning. They are designed to help the kids learn to tune in better and to sustain concentration for longer periods of time. Note that each exercise must begin, minimally, with the steps in the "Capsule Directions." With every exercise, the students should maintain their concentration and deep breathing throughout the entire exercise.

Movie Theatre

Have the students tune in.

"Just concentrate on the flow of your breath and try to block out everything else. [Pause] Imagine you are sitting in an empty movie theatre; you are all alone. [Pause] Feel the hard floor at your feet. Feel the rough cloth of the seat. [Pause] It is very dark and the only thing that you can see is the movie screen. The screen is lit up with blue light. [Pause] Imagine a giant picture suddenly appearing on the screen. [Pause] Now, in your heart, say something to God about the picture you saw."

The students remain silent for another minute. The teacher ends the exercise with debriefing.

Melt Your Body

Have the students tune in.

"As you breathe quietly, feel the muscles in your face and forehead. There will be some stiffness there. Let the muscles in your face just melt away. Pretend they're made of molasses, and they flow slowly downward. [Pause] Feel the muscles around your eyes melt. [Pause] Feel your mouth and jaw melt. [Pause] Now the melting is going on down. Feel your neck melt away. [Pause] It spreads to your shoulders and back. The tension and stiffness just slowly flow downward, leaving you totally relaxed. [Pause] Feel your stomach. Let the tension melt away. [Pause] Feel your arms and hands. The tension melts downward, into your hands and out through the tips of your fingers. [Pause] Feel your hips. Let them melt. [Pause] Feel your legs. All the stiffness flows downward into your feet. [Pause] Feel your whole body. Any tension just flows on down into your feet and out through your toes. [Pause] When you are totally melted, just rest and concentrate on your breathing."

The students remain silent for another minute. The teacher ends the exercise with debriefing.

Jesus Prayer: Short Version

Have the students tune in.

"Each time you breathe in, think the word, 'Jesus.' Each time you breathe out, think the words, 'Come to me.' Keep breathing in and out, concentrating on your breath and the words."

17

The students remain silent for another two minutes. The teacher ends the exercise with debriefing.

Float Away

Have the students tune in.

"Each time you breathe in, imagine that your body gets a little lighter. [Pause] Finally, you become weightless, and drift up off of the floor into the air. [Pause] As you continue to concentrate on your breathing, just float in the air and rest."

The students remain silent for another two minutes. The teacher ends the exercise with debriefing.

Hawaiian Punch

For this exercise, the teacher must bring in a piece of fresh fruit for each student. These should be hidden away from them. It is more fun to have various kinds of fruit. After the students have tuned in, the teacher tells them that each is about to be given an object to hold. They are not to look at it, but simply to hold it in their hands and wait for further instructions. The teacher gives each kid a piece of fruit.

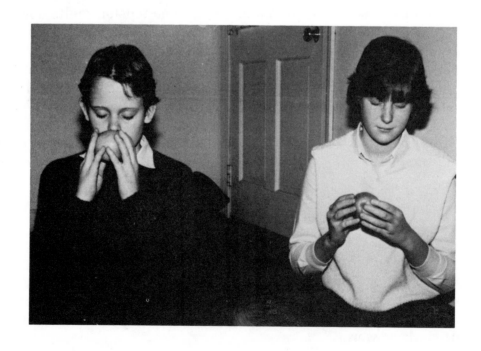

"Now go back to concentrating on your breathing and get very quiet. [Pause] Feel the object in your hands very carefully. Be extremely gentle. Treat it as though it were very fragile. Feel every part of it slowly and gently. [Pause for one minute] Just with your sense of touch, get to know the object so well you can pick it out from a group of others just like it. [Pause] Without changing your breathing, slowly lift the object to your nose and breathe in its smell. [Pause] Now, in your heart, thank God for the wonderful thing he has made."

The students remain silent for another minute. The teacher ends the exercise with debriefing. The students eat their fruit.

Fantasy Prayers

Middle school kids love to fantasize, especially if they can imagine themselves to be in the very center of the action. Their love of fantasy can be used to help them to pray. Fantasy often helps people get in touch with their unconscious feelings, desires, or fears. Once these are allowed to seep to the surface, they can become occasions for deep and meaningful prayer.

The following exercises are designed to take advantage of the middle school student's natural inclination to engage in fantasizing. Each one helps the students enter into a fantasy, and then to pray about their experience. The creative teacher may use these fifteen examples as a pattern, and design other fantasy prayers for the kids.

Climb Every Mountain

Have the students tune in.

"Imagine that you are standing at the bottom of a giant mountain. When you look up at the top you have to bend your neck far back. [Pause] You see a small, winding path in front of you and you begin to climb up the mountain. [Pause] The path is steep; you begin to pant and your legs hurt. [Pause] You look down and see that you have climbed a long way up. Your heart pounds. You continue climbing. [Pause] Suddenly, you see a valuable object lying in the path. You pick it up; you are excited to find it. [Pause] As you climb, you suddenly trip and fall. You hurt your knee, and it bleeds. The pain goes deep into the bone, and you want to cry. [Pause] But the top of the mountain is close, now, and you keep going. [Pause] Finally, you are at the top. You look down, and it is so high. Everything below seems tiny. The cool wind blows all around. [Pause] You hear a little noise, turn around, and see Jesus standing there. You say hello. [Pause]

You show Jesus your valuable object and tell him all about it. [Pause] He answers you."

The students remain silent for another minute. The teacher ends the exercise by debriefing.

Lighten My Load, Lord

Have the students tune in.

"Imagine that you are carrying a terribly heavy box. Your back aches and you are panting and sweating. [Pause] Your hands really hurt. You are having a hard time keeping your grip on the box. [Pause] Just when you are about to give up and drop it, Jesus comes and helps you carry the box."

The students remain silent for one minute. The teacher ends the exercise by debriefing.

The Robinson Crusoe Encounter

Have the students tune in.

"Imagine that you are walking all alone on a huge beach on a desert island. As far as you can see the sand and waters stretch out. It is lonely. [Pause] Feel the wind blowing on your face. Smell the salty air. [Pause] See and hear the waves washing up onto the sand. [Pause] Look up at the bright blue sky. Do you see any clouds? The seagulls are circling overhead, crying out to one another. [Pause] Begin to walk down the beach. If you see anything you want to pick up, pick it up and hold it. [Pause] Look 'way down the beach; a person is approaching you. The person is so far away that you cannot see who it is, or even whether it is a man, woman, or child. [Pause] As you walk, the person is getting closer and looking larger and larger. Finally you are able to tell that it is a man. [Pause] When you get even closer, you recognize the man: it is Jesus. [Pause] He joins you and both of you continue walking down the beach in the same direction. Imagine what you talk about. [Pause] Now thank Jesus for meeting you on the beach."

The students remain silent for another minute. The teacher ends the exercise by debriefing.

Fly Away!

This exercise requires the use of music. A selection of music which is exultant and lilting, and which is five to ten minutes in length, is best. "The Blue Danube Waltz" by Johann Strauss is particularly well suited. The teacher may find other equally suitable selections.

Have the students tune in.

"Imagine yourself standing all alone on a high mountain peak. [Pause] Below you on the left you see a desert valley, all dry and hot, with lots of sand. [Pause] Below you on your right, you see a beautiful green forest, filled with trees and animals. [Pause] As you stand on the peak, the winds are strong. They make your clothes flap against your body. [Pause] You stretch out your arms, and as you begin to hear the music play, you take off and fly."

The music is played using plenty of volume. When it is over, the teacher pauses a moment and concludes the exercise by debriefing.

Desert Rescue

Have the students tune in.

"Imagine yourself walking all alone across a huge desert. As far as you can see in all directions there is nothing but sand. [Pause] The sun is incredibly bright and hurts your eyes. Feel the hot sun on your head and the hot sand beneath your feet. [Pause] You are terribly thirsty. Your tongue is swollen and has turned blue in color. It sticks to your mouth and throat and feels as though it will choke you. [Pause] You feel weaker and weaker. The sun burns your skin. You can hardly breathe in air. Finally, you can't walk any farther. You fall down. [Pause] You are dying. [Pause] After a while you look up and see a man coming toward you. He is far away. [Pause] As he gets closer, you recognize him. It is Jesus. [Pause] Jesus gives you a drink of water. [Pause] He picks you up and begins to carry you. You feel his strong arms around your body as he holds you up. [Pause] Imagine what you would say to Jesus as he carries you and what he might answer."

The students remain silent for another two minutes. The teacher ends the exercise by debriefing.

Bombs Away!

Have the students tune in.

"Pretend you are a skydiver. You are riding 'way up in a little single engine airplane. [Pause] You look out the open door and see the earth far below; the fields look like a patchwork quilt. You hear the buzz of the little engine and the roar of the wind. [Pause] The air smells so clean it's almost unreal. Your helmet and parachute pack and boots make you feel very heavy. [Pause] It is time. You stand in the open doorway, looking out into the sky. You know that after you jump you will have three minutes to fall freely before you must open your parachute. [Pause] You leap out into space. The ground seems to be very still; it's hard to tell that it's coming closer to you. You hear only the wind, the flapping of your jumpsuit, and the pounding of your heart. [Pause for one and one half minutes.] Now you are halfway down. You just float along. You are all alone with God. [Pause for one and one half minutes.] Now you open your parachute. As you drift on down to the ground, speak to God about your experience."

The students remain silent for another minute. The teacher ends the exercise by debriefing.

He Is Risen!

This is a good meditation to use with the kids during the Easter season.

Have the students tune in.

"Imagine that it is just three days after Jesus has died. You have gone for a walk by yourself. Where are you walking? [Pause] Think about your dead friend Jesus while you walk. [Pause] How do you feel? What do you wish? [Pause] All of a sudden, Jesus appears to you. [Pause] How do you feel now? [Pause] What do you say to Jesus? What does he answer? [Pause] Now take a minute to pray to Jesus about his resurrection."

The students remain silent for another minute. The teacher ends the exercise by debriefing.

The Enchanted Forest

Have the students tune in.

"Imagine that you are walking down a road beside a very beautiful forest. The trees are a lush green. It is a sunny day, very pretty out. [Pause] To your right you see a little path that enters the forest. You wait a moment, and then begin to walk down the path. [Pause] You walk on and on, winding your way among the beautiful trees. Overhead you hear hundreds of birds singing. [Pause] You come to a creek. The clear, cool water bubbles over the rocks. You stoop and take a long drink. [Pause] Instead of following the path, you follow the creek. [Pause] After a while you see a beaver dam. You are very quiet. You can see the beavers working on the dam. [Pause] There is a hill ahead of you. You go that way, and begin to climb up it. [Pause] The hill is steep. You are panting. Your legs hurt. [Pause] Near the top of the hill, to your left, you see the black entrance of a cave. You slowly go over to it. It is dark inside. [Pause] You begin to edge your way into the cave, step by step. It is too dark to see. [Pause] You turn around and look at the entrance. You are surprised at how far away it seems to be. [Pause] Suddenly you see something in the darkness that really scares you. You panic and run out of the cave as fast as you can. [Pause] You run and run through the woods. The branches whip past and scratch your face. You stumble and fall. [Pause] You get up and look around. You are breathing hard. All you can see is trees. [Pause] There is no creek. There is no path. There is no hill. You are lost. [Pause] You sit down and begin to cry, because you are afraid. [Pause] After a while you hear footsteps. They sound like a person's. [Pause] He approaches; it is Jesus. [Pause] Jesus tells you that he will take you back to the road. [Pause] While you walk, take a minute and tell Jesus about what scared you in the cave."

The students remain silent for another minute. The teacher ends the exercise by debriefing.

Blast Off!

Have the students tune in.

"Imagine that you are in a space capsule on top of a giant rocket at Cape Canaveral. You are going to be the first person to be sent to a strange planet. [Pause] The blast off takes place. There is a roar of fire and smoke. [Pause] You head into outer space, traveling at the speed of light. Behind you, the earth grows small, then disappears completely. [Pause] After a few hours, your radio contact with mission control ceases. You are too far away for the radio. [Pause] Up ahead, you see your planet. It is getting closer. [Pause] You begin to orbit the planet. You climb into your space shuttle, leave the main capsule, and ride down to the surface of the planet. [Pause] It is a desert wasteland. You get out of your shuttle. As far as you can see in all directions, there is sand and rock. [Pause] You begin to walk around and explore. Your instruments tell you that there is no life on this planet: no plants, no animals, nothing. [Pause] There is not even a wind. Just sand and rocks, rocks and sand, as far as your eyes can see. [Pause] You have never in your life been more alone. There is no one to talk to. There are no sounds. There is just you. [Pause] You are totally alone. [Pause] Take a moment to tell God how it feels to be totally alone. Ask him to be with you."

The students remain silent for another minute. The teacher ends the exercise by debriefing.

Me and Jesus

This is a wonderful meditation exercise which I have borrowed from the Sulpician Fathers. It is very durable, and can be repeated on many different occasions with good results. It should be part of the kids' standard repertoire of prayer.

Have the students tune in.

"Picture Jesus standing in front of you; look deeply into his eyes. [Pause for one minute.] Picture Jesus in your heart; feel his love for you. [Pause for one minute.] Picture Jesus in your hands; what does he ask you to do?" [Pause for one minute.]

The teacher ends the exercise by debriefing. A worthwhile follow-up is to have students write down any insights they have, especially about what Jesus is asking them to do.

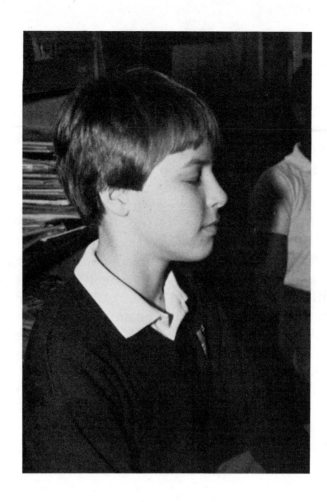

My Hero (Or Heroine)

Have the students tune in.

"Think of your favorite movie or television hero or heroine. Not the actor or actress, but the character that the person pretends to be. [Pause] See your hero. Imagine how he or she looks. Hear the sound of his or her voice. [Pause] Now pretend that you are going to the place where your hero lives. [Pause] You meet the person. The two of you begin to talk. [Pause] Your hero takes you around to see some things. [Pause] You decide that you would like to tell your hero about Jesus, and what Jesus means to you. You hope that your hero will believe in Jesus, too. Take a minute to tell your hero all about Jesus."

The students remain silent for another minute. The teacher ends the exercise by debriefing.

The Biggest Secret in the World

Have the students tune in.

"Pretend that you are sitting with Jesus. The two of you are facing each other. Imagine how Jesus looks. [Pause] What color is his hair? How about his eyes? Does he have a beard? [Pause] What is Jesus wearing? [Pause] Tell Jesus a secret of yours. You may think he knows about it already, but tell him anyway. [Pause] Now Jesus says that he is going to tell you the biggest secret in the world, a secret that no one else knows. He tells you. [Pause for thirty seconds.] Now take a minute and discuss this big secret with Jesus. Tell him what you think about it, and ask him any questions you have."

The students remain silent for another minute. The teacher ends the exercise by debriefing.

When It Rains, It Pours!

This exercise requires the use of a sound recording of a rainstorm, preferably with thunder. Such recordings are available at most record stores and many libraries.

Have the students tune in.

"Listen now for a few minutes to the sound of the rainstorm. Let the sounds sink deeply into your heart and soul. Try to become one with the sound, so that you *are* the sound and the sound is you. As you listen, think about what these sounds tell you about God."

The sound recording is played for about five minutes.

"Now tell God how you feel."

The students remain silent for another minute. The teacher ends the exercise by debriefing.

Exciting variations to the above exercise may be created by using sound recordings of other natural things: a running stream, a hurricane, the wind blowing through the trees, insects chirping, whale songs, etc.

Your Sea Is So Great,
and My Boat Is So Small!

Have the students tune in.

"Imagine that you are getting into a small wooden rowboat at the edge of the ocean. Your boat is about twelve feet long. It is made of rough, gray wood. [Pause] There are a couple of bench-like seats in the boat. There are two oars. There is nothing else. [Pause] You begin to row away from the shore and out into the sea. You row and row. [Pause] You are surprised at how fast you move away from the shore. The waves are light, and soon the shore disappears into the horizon. [Pause] You stand in your boat and look around you. All you see on every side is water. [Pause] Suddenly clouds begin to cover the sun. The waves grow larger and larger. [Pause] Your little boat begins to toss wildly about. You can't see the shore, and you don't even know which way it is anymore. [Pause] You are totally lost and out of control. You cry out to God, 'Your sea is so great, and my boat is so small!' [Pause] Take a minute now, and keep repeating that to God, over and over: 'Your sea is so great, and my boat is so small!' "

The students remain silent for another minute. The teacher ends the exercise by debriefing.

Nature Valley

This exercise is designed to help the students appreciate God's creation and thank him for it. A sound recording of soft and gentle music is required.

Have the students tune in.

"Imagine the prettiest nature scene that you have ever seen, either in person or in a movie, TV show, or picture. Try to hear, smell, and touch every part of it. Pretend that you are right in the middle of it."

The background music is played for about five minutes.

"Thank God for making such a beautiful world and for sharing part of it with you."

The students remain silent for another minute. The teacher ends the meditation by debriefing.

The Three R's: Remember, Review, and Reflect

The most profound and meaningful prayer is that which relates to real life experience. After all, prayer is all about our relationship with God, and that relationship takes place in our daily lives. Sometimes when kids are trying to pray, they need "grist for the mill." Providing that grist is the first goal of the following exercises.

But there is a second need which these exercises strive to meet. People need a chance to take a step back from the whirlwind of life every once in a while. It's sort of like stepping off the merry-go-round for a bit. Taking a step back helps us see where our lives are going. It helps us to see the forest as well as the trees. Some people make retreats for this purpose. But on a more day to day level, "tiny retreats" are needed. These exercises can be used as "tiny retreats" which give the participants a few moments to stop the action and take stock of life. They will help the kids to examine different aspects of their lives and to pray about that.

Wake Up!

Have the students tune in.

"Think back to this morning when you first woke up. Imagine yourself lying in bed. [Pause] Try to remember what your first thoughts of the day were. What was going on in your mind as you drifted out of sleep into wakefulness? [Pause for one minute.] Take a minute now and say something to God about your first thoughts today."

The students remain silent for another minute. The teacher ends the exercise by debriefing, including these questions:

- Did you have any trouble remembering your first thoughts?

- Were your first thoughts important and serious, or unimportant, maybe even silly?

- Many people find that they can pray well when they first wake up in the morning. How about you?

A Variation: Go through the same exercise, but have the students focus on their last thoughts of the day as they drifted off to sleep the night before.

One Day at a Time

This is a wonderful bedtime prayer for all people. It helps you to take a step back from the hustle and bustle of daily life and see where you are going. This sort of prayer is a powerful aid to discerning God's activity in your life and his will for you. The students should be taught this technique and encouraged to do it every night before they go to sleep.

Have the students tune in.

"Think back over the last twenty-four hours. What was happening to you yesterday at just this time? [Pause] What happened at lunchtime? [Here the teacher must select appropriate time periods. If this exercise is being done in the morning, the teacher should work through the rest of the day and night. If this exercise is being done at night, the teacher must focus the students on the previous night and the events of the current day. Choose about five time periods in sequence for the students to recollect.] Now take a minute to speak to God about the last day. Tell him what you learned, and whether you felt that he was with you."

The students remain silent for another minute. The teacher ends the exercise by debriefing.

Variations: Pick any other appropriate length of time to recall and reflect upon. This exercise could be done on a regular basis—weekly, monthly, etc. Longer reflection periods are appropriate for longer periods of time.

Finding Time for God

Have the students tune in.

"Imagine waking up in the morning. You are lying in bed. Light is coming through your bedroom window. [Pause] Imagine being in school in the morning. What class are you in? Where are you seated? Who else is there? [Pause] Imagine lunchtime. It is noisy. What's for lunch? [Pause] Imagine the afternoon at school. What are you doing now? What time is it? Are you anxious to leave? [Pause] Imagine being at home, waiting for dinner. Who is doing the cooking? What are you doing? Are your parents home? [Pause] Imagine the time from dinner until you go to bed. What are you doing? Homework? Watching TV? Getting a shower or putting on pajamas? [Pause] Imagine lying in bed. The covers are warm. Is there much light in the room? What sounds do you hear? What are you thinking about? [Pause] Now think of all those times, and tell Jesus which times you think are the best ones for you to pray."

The students remain silent for two more minutes. The teacher ends the exercise by debriefing.

34

I Am Loved

Have the students tune in.

"As you meditate, think of different ways that God has shown his love for you. [Pause for one minute.] What are the most important ways? [Pause] Are some of the ways that God shows his love for you hard to accept? [Pause] Tell God how you feel about his love. [Pause] If there are other ways that you want God to love you, tell him about that, too."

The students remain silent for another minute. The teacher ends the exercise by debriefing.

When I Was Hungry . . .

This exercise provides a way for the students to reflect upon any charitable activities with which they have been involved. Most school or religious education programs provide some kind of service opportunities for the students. (If yours does not, shame on you!) These should be recalled with the students before the meditation begins, and the memory should be made as concrete as possible. In addition, students may share other ways in which they have helped others in the past few months. When enough remembering and sharing has been done, have the students tune in.

"Listen to these words of Jesus. As you hear his words, think about the things that you have done for other people who needed you. You might think about class projects, or about things that you have done with your family or on your own."

Matthew 25:31–40 (When I was hungry . . .) is read slowly and carefully.

"Is there just one more thing that Jesus might want you to do?"

The students remain silent for another minute. The teacher ends the exercise by debriefing.

Help!

This is a good exercise to use when the students are under stress: before tests or exam periods, when they are working hard on a special project or term paper, etc.

Have the students tune in.

"Think about the things that will challenge you in the next few days [or hours, or minutes]. Think of each of them, one by one, and make a little mental list as you go. [Pause for one minute] How are you feeling as you sit and think of these things? Are you a little nervous or scared? [Pause] Now tell God about each thing on your list, and ask for his help."

The students remain silent for another two minutes. The teacher ends the exercise by debriefing.

Holiday's Over!

This may be used at the first class meeting after the students return from Christmas vacation.

Have the students tune in.

"Think back to Christmas Eve. What things were happening that day? [Pause] Where were you? Who was with you? What was the mood? [Pause] Think about Christmas Day. What were the big events for you? What were the big events for others? [Pause] What was your main feeling on Christmas Day? [Pause] Remember the week after Christmas. What things were you doing? Did you see any relatives or friends? [Pause] Was it fun? [Pause] Now thank God for all of the good things that happened to you on vacation. [Pause] Was there anything bad that happened during your vacation? If there was, tell God about it."

The students remain silent for another minute. The teacher ends the exercise by debriefing.

Variations of this exercise may be used after any vacation period. The key is to help the kids to remember the events and the feelings that were associated with them. Don't make them do a "whitewash." Even Christmas vacation can be a terrible experience for some people!

My Special People

Have the students tune in.

"All of us have special people in our lives. Sometimes we might have just a couple. Sometimes we are lucky enough to have lots of special people. [Pause] Think of your special people, the ones you love the most. Think of them one by one, and picture them sitting or standing right in front of you. Picture each one for a moment before you move on to the next person. [Pause for one or two minutes.] Now go back through your list of special people again. As you picture each one, tell God what you love or admire most about that person. Then thank God for giving you the gift of your special person."

The students remain silent for another two minutes. The teacher ends the exercise by debriefing.

Love Your Enemy

Have the students tune in.

"Most of us have enemies, or at least people we don't like. Maybe they were mean to us sometime. Maybe we actually had a big fight. Maybe they just don't like us, or we just don't like them. [Pause] Take a minute now, and try to think of the people who are your enemies, or at least the people you don't like. Imagine each of them, and picture what it is about them that you don't like. [Pause for one or two minutes.] Now go back through the list again. Each time you imagine a person you don't like, tell God what it is you don't like about that person. Then ask God to bless that person, and ask God to help you to like him or her."

The students remain silent for another two minutes. The teacher ends the exercise by debriefing, including these questions:

- Was it hard to pray for the people you don't like?

- What did Jesus tell us about our enemies?

Green with Envy

Have the students tune in.

"Remember a time when you were envious of another person or jealous about something that person did or had. [Pause] Picture the events in your mind. Play it all out as if you were watching it on television. [Pause for one minute.] How did you feel? [Pause] Did you say anything to the person, or to other people? [Pause] Take a minute now and tell God about that time and what it was like for you to feel jealous. Ask God to help you not to feel so jealous."

The students remain silent for another minute. The teacher ends the exercise by debriefing.

I'm Hurt!

Have the students tune in.

"Remember a time when you had an accident and got hurt. [Pause] What events led up to your accident? Where did it take place? [Pause] Picture the accident actually happening, as if you were watching it on TV. [Pause] Are you bleeding? Is something broken? Are there bruises? [Pause] Remember the pain you felt. [Pause] How did you feel? Were you frightened? Angry? [Pause] Take a moment to tell God about what happened, and what it felt like to be hurt."

The students remain silent for another minute. The teacher ends the exercise by debriefing.

The Lord Is My Shepherd

Have the students tune in.

"Remember a time when you were in some kind of danger. Maybe it was a great danger, like the danger of being killed, or maybe it was a smaller danger, like the danger of being hurt. [Pause] Where was this? What was happening at the time? [Pause] Were there any people with you, or were you all alone? [Pause] Play the dangerous events through in your mind. Visualize them as if you were watching it all on television. [Pause for one minute.] Take a moment now and thank God for protecting you at that time. Ask God always to be with you and to protect you."

The students remain silent for another minute. The teacher ends the exercise by debriefing.

Me, the Great!

Have the students tune in.

"Recall the greatest accomplishment of your whole life. What was your life's greatest moment? [Pause] When did this take place? Where? [Pause] Picture yourself at the time. How old were you? What did you look like? [Pause] Did you have an audience, or was this a more private achievement? [Pause] Replay your accomplishment through in your mind as if you were watching it on TV. Take your time and enjoy the memory. [Pause for one or two minutes.] Now take a minute to thank God for your great moment. Ask him to help you have more great moments in your life."

The students remain silent for another minute. The teacher ends the exercise by debriefing.

A Good Ending

This exercise is designed to be used at the end of the school year. It will help the kids to review their year and pray about it. Five minutes or so of soft background music is required.

Have the students tune in.

"Think back over our work together this school year. What was your greatest moment this year? [Pause] Why was that the greatest moment for you? What made it so special? [Pause] What was your worst moment? [Pause] How did you feel then? [Pause] Think about your prayer life and what you have learned. What is your best way to pray? What kinds of prayer bring you closest to God? [Pause for one minute.] Now tell God about how you think he wants you to pray."

The students remain silent for another minute. The teacher ends the exercise by debriefing.

Musical Prayers

Music provides a powerful means of stimulating the kids' interest and getting a message across to them. The exercises in this section make use of songs and musical selections which are available for purchase in most record stores. Using the patterns presented here, and taking *great* care in selection, the teacher may find more contemporary music which can be used effectively for prayer and meditation. The kids will be thrilled to find out that one of their favorite songs on the radio can enhance their spiritual lives. Most of the songs suggested in the following exercises were "Top 40's" in their day.

When using music for meditation exercise, it is most important that the quality of sound be as high as possible. Old, scratchy records or tiny little cassette players have a deadly effect. Every effort should be made to use machinery which delivers good quality sound at sufficient volume. For the most part, music should be played loudly; the kids are accustomed to very loud music, and what seems deafening to many adults is normal for the kids. Don't be stingy with the volume!

Preparation of the machinery and recording is very important. Records should be cleaned and the needle should be placed beforehand at the beginning of the song. It is distracting for the teacher to try three or four times to drop the needle onto the proper place on the record. Record players with a "pause" control are very helpful. The teacher should experiment before the kids arrive in order to find the proper volume and tone settings for the music which will be used. During the meditation exercise, when the music comes to an end, the machine should be cut off as quietly as possible to avoid loud "clicks" or other noises. Often it is better quickly to turn the volume to "0" than to try to shut off the machine or remove the needle from the record.

A final word of warning: much popular music is distinctly *not* appropriate for instilling Christian values or for aiding prayer. Sometimes teachers, in an attempt to be "relevant" or "in touch," sacrifice good taste or sound doctrine and morals. Don't fall into that trap!

Simple Pleasures Are the Best

Begin this exercise by explaining to the students that there is a giant "pleasure industry" in our country. Amusement parks, arcades, travel companies, etc., all sell pleasurable experiences. Have the students help list some examples of pleasure for sale. Then explain that all of this emphasis on pleasure can cause us to forget life's simple pleasures which can't be bought, and that, in fact, simple pleasures are the best.

The students need a pencil and a piece of paper for this exercise.

Have the students tune in.

"Listen now to this song about simple pleasures. See how many simple pleasures you can hear about."

"Poems, Prayers & Promises" by John Denver (from the album *Poems, Prayers & Promises* [New York: RCA Records, 1971]) is played.

"Now take your pencil and paper and make a list of your simple pleasures. Think of as many as you can. [The students work in silence for two or three minutes.] Now read over your list, and thank God for giving you each of those simple pleasures."

The students remain silent for another minute. The teacher ends the exercise by debriefing.

Floating in Space

Have the students tune in. Tell them that the exercise will last about ten minutes.

"Imagine yourself floating in outer space. You are weightless. [Pause] All around, you see the dark background and little pinpoints of light which are stars. [Pause] It is absolutely silent. You are all alone with God. While this music plays, imagine yourself floating in space with God."

A ten minute selection of Gregorian chant is played. The teacher ends the exercise by debriefing.

A Variation: While the same music is played, have the students imagine a beautiful room, filled with light, where they meet God.

"Bridge Over Troubled Water"

Love has many faces. It can be challenging, supportive, demanding, passionate, tranquil, dangerous, healing, soothing, hurtful, etc. Love, whether between two persons, or between one person and God, is very complex and can be difficult to understand. This exercise focuses on one aspect of love that middle school kids especially crave: being loved helps a person to feel safe and secure. The love described in this beautiful song is an especially apt metaphor for God's love for us.

After explaining the above to the students, have them tune in.

"Listen carefully to this love song. See if it tells you anything about God's love for you."

"Bridge Over Troubled Water" by Simon and Garfunkel (from the album *Bridge Over Troubled Water* [New York: Columbia Records]) is played.

"Now tell God what his love means to you. You may want to thank him for loving you."

The students remain silent for another two minutes. The teacher ends the exercise by debriefing.

Be Not Afraid

All of us have one thing or another, more often many things, that make us afraid. People, places, situations, expectations, etc., can all be frightening. The good news of Jesus Christ is that we no longer have to be afraid: God is with us and has already saved us. The aim of this meditation exercise is to help the students hear on a deeper level God's loving reassurance.

Have the students tune in.

"Imagine that you are afraid. You might remember something that actually happened that was scary, or you might imagine something that you are afraid will happen. [Pause] God helps us when we are afraid. Listen carefully to the words of this song. Pretend that these words are coming to you from God himself. Let every word soak into your heart."

"Be Not Afraid" by the St. Louis Jesuits (from the album *Earthen Vessels* [Phoenix: North American Liturgy Resources, 1975]) is played.

"Now say something to God about those words."

The students remain silent for another minute. The teacher ends the exercise by debriefing.

My Wedding Day

This exercise makes an excellent introduction or conclusion to a teaching session about the sacrament of matrimony.

Have the students tune in.

"Imagine yourself on your wedding day. You are all dressed up in fine clothes. You and your loved one look so nice and so happy and excited. [Pause] Look at all the guests who have come to see you be married. They are your family and best friends, the people you love most. [Pause] Imagine your loved one. How does he or she look? [Pause] Listen to this wedding song, and dream about your own wedding day."

"Wedding Song" by Paul Stookey (from the album *Paul and* [New York: Warner Bros. Records 1971]) is played.

"Take a minute now to speak to God about your wedding. Tell him how the song made you feel."

The students remain silent for another minute. The teacher ends the exercise by debriefing. Special questions to ask include:

- What does it mean to be two people gathered in God's name?
- When two people are getting married, is God especially close to them? How?
- Do you think God approves of marriage?
- Not all people are called to marriage by God. Some are called by God to stay single. What do you think God will call you to do?

"7 O'Clock News/Silent Night"

This exercise is useful for helping the students to develop a deeper awareness of social needs in the world around them. For those insulated in upper or middle class environments, human strife and suffering may seem unreal. Not only does this song raise consciousness, it challenges the listener to step out of his or her cocoon.

Have the students tune in.

"Listen carefully to this song. It will surprise you. It is not what it seems to be at first. The song has a definite message for you. See if you can figure it out."

"7 O'Clock News/Silent Night" by Simon and Garfunkel (on the album *Parsley, Sage, Rosemary and Thyme* [New York: Columbia Records]) is played.

"Now take a moment to speak to God about the message that you heard."

The students remain silent for another minute. The teacher ends the exercise by debriefing.

Whatsoever You Do . . .

The students need a pencil and a piece of paper for this exercise.

Have the students tune in.

"This song is like a fable. Remember, a fable is a story, usually about animals, which has a message to tell. The message of this song is very clear. Listen to it carefully."

"Sparrow" by Simon and Garfunkel (from the album *Wednesday Morning, 3 A.M.* [New York: Columbia Records]) is played.

"Now take your pencil and paper and write a note to God about the moral of this story."

The students work for two or three minutes. When they seem to be finished, the teacher ends the exercise by debriefing.

To Be Old

We live in a society where youth is extolled and age is often feared. The kids constantly watch television where people are shown to be horrified to find wrinkles and gray hairs, and where older people are so often depicted in derogatory ways: they are shown to be foolish, weak, out of touch with reality, cute, and usually harmless. In addition, it seems as though our whole society attempts to deny aging. Hair dyes, wrinkle removers, "age spot" creams, etc., enjoy a booming business. The world is filled with people who keep their true age a secret, or who try to act decades younger than they actually are. This denial of aging makes it all the more difficult for middle school kids to face up to their own mortality; yet an awareness of one's own mortality and finitude is essential in order to have a mature spiritual life.

This exercise is designed to help. The teacher would do well to precede it with some teaching about aging, with a special effort being made to counter the negative feelings and denial which our culture so often associates with old age.

Have the students tune in. Two selections by Simon and Garfunkel, "Voices of Old People" and "Old Friends" (on the album *Bookends* [New York: Columbia Records]), are played without pause in between.

"Imagine yourself being old. Imagine how you must look. [Pause] Your hair is white, your skin is wrinkled. You don't stand up as straight as you used to. [Pause] Imagine how your body feels. Your muscles and bones aren't as strong as they used to be. Maybe you have trouble seeing clearly. Your hearing might not be so good, either. [Pause] Do you have any sicknesses? Do you have to take medicines every day? Can you take care of yourself? [Pause] Now take a minute or two and speak to God about being old."

The students remain silent for one or two more minutes. The teacher ends the exercise by debriefing.

A Variation: Have the students visit older people, whether in their homes, or in a nursing home. Then, in the meditation exercise, ask them to visualize older people they actually met rather than themselves being old.

Another Variation: After the exercise, have the students write a poem or story or essay about what it is like to be old.

"Joy Was Just the Thing That He Was Raised On"

Our faith in Jesus Christ should be a source of great joy. Often kids don't realize that, particularly if they have learned to view church attendance and religious education as boring duties, devoid of excitement or relevance. Ask them if their faith ever makes them happy or gives them strength when they are sad. See if some of the students are willing to give concrete examples of this from their own lives.

When you feel that they are ready for the prayer exercise, have them tune in.

"This song is about the joy and strength that one person, named Matthew, found in his faith. Listen carefully to the words of this song as they tell the story of Matthew."

"Matthew" by John Denver (on the album *Back Home Again* [New York: RCA Records, 1974]) is played.

"Now think again about whether your faith ever makes you happy or gives you strength. [Pause] Take a minute to tell God about that."

The students remain silent for another minute. The teacher ends the exercise by debriefing.

Stay with Me, Lord

It is often difficult to love another person. Love can be a great challenge, and so often it involves taking risks: Where will my love for another lead me? What will it do to me? What if I lose the person? Will my love hurt me? Our love of God can be the same. When we think of our relationship with God, we have to face those same questions, and many more besides. Discuss these ideas with the kids before doing this exercise.

Have the students tune in.

"This song is about love. It was probably written about love between two human beings, but it could also be about the love between a person and God. Listen carefully and think about whether you have ever felt the way the singer feels in this song."

"Follow Me" by John Denver (from the album *John Denver's Greatest Hits* [New York: RCA Records, 1973]) is played.

"Take a minute now and speak to God about how you feel."

The students remain silent for another minute. The teacher ends the exercise by debriefing. In addition to the usual things covered, the following questions may be added:

- Has it ever been hard for you to love God?
- Has your love for God changed you in any way?
- Do you think the singer in that song will keep on loving?

They Have Killed the Lord!

This meditation exercise helps the students to imagine more vividly the crucifixion of Jesus.

Have the students tune in.

"This recording will help you imagine the crucifixion of Jesus. As you listen, pretend that you are really there. Let every sound sink deeply into your heart and help you to picture what is happening."

"The Crucifixion" from the rock opera *Jesus Christ Superstar,* by Andrew Lloyd Weber and Tim Rice (New York: Decca Records, 1970) is played, followed immediately by "John Nineteen Forty-One," which is the next band on the record.

The students remain silent for another minute. The teacher ends the exercise by debriefing.

A Variation: The "Finale" from the Broadway musical *Godspell* (New York: Bell Records) is played. This music is more abstract than the fairly literal version from *Jesus Christ Superstar,* and the students should be warned of this beforehand.

He Is Not Here!

Have the students tune in.

"Imagine that Jesus has died a couple of days ago. You are walking to his tomb. [Pause] You feel very sad and frightened about his death. It seems as if everything he said meant nothing after all. [Pause] Up ahead is the hill where they dug out the tomb. You can see the giant rock that was placed over the opening. [Pause] Something doesn't seem right. The rock seems crooked. You hurry along. [Pause] As you get near the tomb, you see that the rock has been pushed aside. The black hole of the opening is visible. [Pause] Suddenly, you see something new. There are dozens of angels around the tomb, all dressed in white. Some look like men and some look like women. They begin to sing."

The Hallelujah Chorus from Handel's *Messiah* is played. When the music is over, the students remain silent for a moment. The teacher ends the exercise by debriefing.

Scriptural Prayers

The use of Sacred Scripture as an aid to prayer is an old and venerable Christian tradition. Simple devotional reading has a great value, but a deeper and more fulfilling way to pray the Scriptures is to identify oneself with the characters and situations described. One of the greatest spiritual masters, St. Ignatius Loyola, was an expert at this technique. In his *Spiritual Exercises,* especially in the Second, Third, and Fourth Weeks, he describes detailed methods which can help the reader learn to identify with biblical characters, and thereby to relive the greatest stories and events of our religious heritage. The *Spiritual Exercises* are an important source for the teacher to consult.

In an excellent discussion of the Stations of the Cross, John Macquarrie points out that there are three levels on which one may identify with biblical events. These correspond to the three basic movements of spiritual growth. First, there is the purgative level, or a person's turning away from sin. In order to turn away from sin, a person must become aware of the sin present in his or her life. Identifying with sinful characters in Bible stories, such as Pilate, Mary Magdalene,

or Peter, can help people to become more attuned to their own sinfulness. The second level is the illuminative: here a person learns to be a disciple of Jesus. Identifying with believers in Jesus, such as disciples, Mary Magdalene, and especially his mother, Mary, can help people learn to follow Jesus and his teachings, just as others have learned before. Finally, there is the unitive level: here, one is able to achieve a sense of unity with Christ. This is the peak of Christian spirituality. Identifying with Jesus in various stories can help a person pick up his own cross and share in the paschal mystery (*Paths in Spirituality* [New York: Harper & Row, 1972] pp. 112–119).

Most of the meditation exercises which follow in this section are aimed at helping the students to identify with events from the life of Jesus. (No effort has been made to sort out the "historical" from "unhistorical" events. Higher biblical criticism is not especially important here.) In the first five exercises, the biblical material has been rewritten (based on Today's English Version [New York: American Bible Society, 1976]) so that the students may follow it more literally. It would be wise to begin with these exercises in order to accustom the students to this type of meditation. Afterward, a shift may be made to exercises in which a section of Scripture is read as is (although the teacher might want to shift into the present tense to enhance the students' feeling of actually being there). The students should learn to use Bible stories without any rewriting: this will enable them to use this meditation style on their own, whenever they want.

The following exercises are given as examples. There are samples of each of the three levels of identification (purgative, illuminative, and unitive). By using a few of these examples, the teacher can learn the pattern and help to create for the students an endless variety of meaningful meditation experiences. A resource not tapped here is the treasury of stories from the Old Testament and from the Acts of the Apostles. Because the Old Testament stories tend to be repetitive and interspersed with irrelevant material, many will have to be rewritten or rearranged for use in meditation. This would be an interesting project for the students to undertake.

There are many sound recordings of the Bible available on the market or in libraries. An interesting variation for any scriptural meditation exercises would be to play the passage from such a recording rather than to have the teacher read it.

Oral readings of Bible stories used as part of meditation exercises must be of the highest calibre. It generally will not work to have students do the reading. This should be done by the teacher. Preparation ahead of time is essential: the teacher must know the passage "inside-out": he or she must know how to use just the right volume, inflection, and speed for each sentence.

A Poseidon Adventure
(Mark 4:35–41)

Have the students tune in.

"Pretend you are one of Jesus's closest friends. You have spent the day on the edge of the Sea of Galilee, and Jesus wants to take a boat and cross over to the other side. You and some other friends agree, and climb into a tiny fishing boat and start to sail across. [Pause] The boat is little and smells like fish. It jumps around a lot on the waves. [Pause] Jesus lies down to take a nap. [Pause] While he is sleeping, the sky gets dark. The air becomes cool and strong winds blow. [Pause] It begins to rain really hard, and the waves become huge. The boat tosses wildly about. [Pause] Big waves begin to wash over the side of the boat and fill it with water. You are scared to death. [Pause] Suddenly you shout at Jesus, who is still asleep, 'Wake up, Jesus! Don't you care that we are about to drown?' [Pause] Jesus stands up and shouts at the wind, 'Be quiet!' He shouts to the waves, 'Be still!' The wind dies down, and the waves become small and the water becomes very calm. [Pause] Jesus turns to you and says, 'Why are you so scared? Don't you have any faith?' [Pause] But you are still afraid, and so are your friends in the boat. When Jesus isn't listening, one of them whispers, 'Who is this man? Even the wind and the waves obey him!' "

The students remain silent for another minute. The teacher ends the exercise by debriefing.

Water into Wine
(John 2:1–9)

Have the students tune in.

"Pretend you are a servant in a rich man's house. His friend has just gotten married, and he is throwing a huge wedding party. There are many guests, including Jesus and his mother, Mary. [Pause] There are wonderful foods all around. There is also delicious wine, which the guests really like. [Pause] You are busy putting out food and taking care of things. Suddenly you realize that you are out of wine. [Pause] You tell your boss, who becomes very upset. You don't know what to do. [Pause] Out of the corner of your eye, you see Mary talking urgently with Jesus. She comes over and says, 'Do whatever Jesus tells you to do.' [Pause] Near the door are six huge pots. They each hold twenty or thirty gallons, and they are used for washing. Jesus tells you, 'Fill these pots with water.' [Pause] You think he's crazy, but you do it anyway. The water is heavy. It takes a few minutes to fill up the pots. [Pause] Then Jesus says, 'Take some water out now and give it to your boss.' You draw out a cup of water, and it has turned into wine! It is delicious wine, far better than any other! [Pause] Now take a minute and speak to Jesus about this miracle."

The students remain silent for another minute. The teacher ends the exercise by debriefing.

The Devil (Almost) Made Me Do It! *(Luke 4:1–13)*

Have the students tune in.

"This is a story about Jesus. Pretend that you are Jesus and that this is happening to you. Try to live the story as I tell it. [Pause]

"You have gone off in the desert to pray by yourself. You have stayed forty days and forty nights, without food or water. You are very tired and hot. You are more hungry and thirsty than you have ever been before. [Pause]

"Suddenly, the devil appears before you. Imagine how he looks. [Pause] He laughs at you for being so hungry and thirsty. He says, 'If you are God's Son, order this stone to turn into bread.' [Pause] You answer, 'Scripture says, Man cannot live on bread alone.' [Pause] Then the devil takes you up into the sky and shows you all the kingdoms of the world in a single instant. You can see everything. [Pause] 'I will give you all this wealth and all this power,' he says. 'It has all been handed over to me, and I can give it to anyone I choose. All you have to do to get it is worship me.' [Pause] You answer, 'Scripture says, Worship the Lord your God and serve only him!' [Pause] Now the devil takes you to the city of Jerusalem and puts you high on the very top of the temple. He says, 'If you are God's Son, throw yourself down from here. For Scripture says, God will order his angels to take good care of you. It also says, They will hold you up with their hands so that not even your feet will be hurt on the stones.' [Pause] You answer, 'But Scripture also says, You must not put the Lord your God to the test.' [Pause]

"The devil has finished testing you now. He leaves. Now take a minute and say something to Jesus about what it is like to be tempted to do wrong."

The students remain silent for another minute. The teacher ends the exercise by debriefing.

54

My Parents Never Let Me Do Anything!
(Luke 2:41–52)

Have the students tune in.

"This is a story about something that happened to Jesus. As the story is told, pretend that you are Jesus, and that these things are happening to you right now. [Pause]

"You and your mom and dad have just spent a few days in Jerusalem at the Passover festival. It was a big celebration, and you had lots of fun. [Pause] When they were getting ready to leave, you wandered into the temple. There are older men there talking and debating; some of them are teachers. Even though your parents were about to leave, you sit and begin to listen to the men. [Pause] Suddenly you realize that hours have gone by. But you are really interested in what the men are saying. You begin to join the discussion. The men are very surprised at how much you know. [Pause] You are so busy talking, you hardly realize that it is nightfall. You spend the night with one of the men, and return the next morning for more discussions. [Pause] You are having more fun than ever before. It is exciting to be there. You stay another whole night. [Pause] The next day you are at it again. Suddenly, in the middle of a really interesting argument, your parents walk into the temple. They storm over to you. They are furious. [Pause]

"Your mother practically shouts, 'Why have you done this to us? We didn't know where you were! Don't you know how worried we have been?' You feel a little scared. [Pause] You answer, 'Why did you have to look for me? Didn't you know that I had to be in my Father's house?' Your parents look at you very strangely. They don't understand. They look angry, hurt, and confused. [Pause] You realize that you must obey them. You get up and leave the temple to go home again."

The students remain silent another minute. The teacher ends the exercise by debriefing, including this question: Do you think Jesus had problems and arguments with his parents the way regular kids do?

Are You the King of the Jews?
(John 18:33–40; 19:1–16)

Explain to the students that in this exercise they will be asked to imagine that they are Pontius Pilate. They should try to identify with him as much as possible.

Have the students tune in.

"This is the story of your only meeting with Jesus of Nazareth. You are Pontius Pilate, the governor, and the Jewish leaders have brought Jesus to you to be judged. They want you to condemn him to die on the cross. [Pause]

"You go to a courtyard and sit down. Jesus is brought in before you. You ask, 'Are you the king of the Jews?' Jesus replies, 'Does this question come from you or have others told you about me?' You say, 'Do you think I am a Jew? It was your own people and the chief priests who handed you over to me. What have you done?' Jesus says, 'My kingdom does not belong to this world; if my kingdom belonged to this world, my followers would fight to keep me from being handed over to the Jewish authorities. No, my kingdom does not belong here!' [Pause]

"At this point you feel confused, so you ask Jesus again, 'Are you are a king, then?' Jesus answers, 'You say that I am a king. I was born and came into the world for this one purpose, to speak about the truth. Whoever belongs to the truth listens to me.' You feel confused again. You ask, 'What is truth?' [Pause]

"The crowds are getting more angry and they are screaming at you, demanding that you send Jesus to his death. You decide to try a compromise: you order your soldiers to whip Jesus. They also make for him a crown of thorns and put a purple robe on him. Then the soldiers make fun of Jesus, yelling, 'Long live the king of the Jews!' [Pause]

"After Jesus has been whipped, you show him again to the crowds. You hope that they will be satisfied. Instead, they scream even more loudly that you must have Jesus crucified. You shout back, '*You* take him, then, and crucify him yourselves! I find no reason to condemn him to death!' The crowd answers, 'We have a law that says he ought to die because he claimed to be the Son of God.' [Pause]

"Now you are really scared. What if this man really is the Son of God? You ask Jesus 'Where do you come from?' but he will not answer you. You feel angry, and you say, 'Why won't you talk to me? Don't you know I have the authority to set you free, or to have you crucified?' [Pause]

"Jesus answers, 'You have authority over me only because it was given to you by God. So the man who handed me over to you is guilty of a worse sin.' Now

56

you are even more scared. You don't want to have Jesus crucified. [Pause] You try arguing with the crowds, but they will not listen. They just keep shouting that Jesus must be crucified. Finally, you give up. [Pause] You order your guards to take Jesus away and crucify him."

The students remain silent for another minute. The teacher ends the exercise by debriefing. Questions to include are:

- Most people would not want to identify with Pontius Pilate. How did you feel about that?

- Do you think you understand Pontius Pilate any better now?

- You have probably heard the expression, "Don't judge a person until you have walked a mile in his shoes." How does that apply to what you just experienced?

- Did you learn anything about Jesus by doing this?

- Did you learn anything about yourself?

A Variation: Have the students pretend that it is the day after Jesus died and that they are Pontius Pilate. Have them write a diary entry about the confrontation with Jesus.

Another Variation: Have the students write a prayer to God that Pontius Pilate might have prayed after this incident.

Out of Darkness
(Mark 10:46–52)

Darkness and light are fundamental religious symbols, so much so that they barely need explaining. This exercise helps the kids to think about darkness and about the gift of light that Jesus gives them.

Have the students tune in.

"With your eyes closed as they are now, you are surrounded by darkness. Pretend that you are completely unable to open your eyes ever again. [Pause] Hear the sounds around you. Feel the floor beneath you. You will never see these things. [Pause] Now listen to the story I am going to read. Pretend that you are there. If you can, pretend that it is happening to you."

The story of Jesus healing Bartimaeus (Mark 10:46–52) is read slowly, with significant pauses between sentences.

"Now say something to Jesus about what he just did."

The students remain silent for another minute. The teacher ends the exercise by debriefing.

Bread and Fish
(Mark 6:35–44)

Have the students tune in.

"Imagine that you are part of a huge crowd that has been listening to Jesus teach. You have been sitting all day long in the hot sun listening, and you haven't even had a chance to eat. You and the people around you are terribly hungry. [Pause] There is no place to buy food; you are too far out in the country. Your stomach hurts. [Pause] As you listen to the story, imagine that it is really happening to you."

Mark 6:35–44 is read, with significant pauses between the sentences.

"God loves to give us good things. Take a moment to tell him about anything that you might be needing."

The students remain silent for another minute. The teacher ends the exercise by debriefing.

If at First You Don't Succeed
(Mark 8:22–26)

Have the students tune in.

"As you listen to this story, pretend that you are Jesus. Try to imagine how Jesus felt during this event. Try to feel as Jesus must have felt." [Pause]

Mark 8:22–26 is read with significant pauses between the sentences. The students remain silent for another minute. The teacher ends the exercise by debriefing, including the following questions:

- How do you think Jesus felt when the man said that people looked like trees?

- Do you think that it was possible for Jesus to fail? (See Mark 6:1–6.)

Blessed Are You!
(Matthew 5:3–12)

Have the students tune in.

"Picture Jesus sitting in front of you. He is very close. [Pause] What does he look like? How long is his hair? What color is it? [Pause] What is Jesus wearing? [Pause] Look deeply into his eyes. Feel as close to Jesus as you can. [Pause] Now as you hear these words of Jesus, imagine that he is actually saying them directly to you."

The Beatitudes (Matthew 5:3–12) are read slowly, with a significant pause after each one.

"Which of those sayings that you just heard is your favorite? [Pause] Repeat your favorite saying to yourself once or twice, and then speak to Jesus about why that is your favorite."

The students remain silent for another minute. The teacher ends the exercise by debriefing. The students may be invited to share with the group their favorite Beatitude, and why it is particularly meaningful to them.

A Variation: Use this same technique of visualizing Jesus, and read one or more parables instead of the Beatitudes. This may be repeated on numerous occasions, using different biblical material each time.

Footwashing
(John 13:1–17)

Have the students tune in.

"Pretend that you are Peter. It is the night before Jesus will be killed. You have gathered with Jesus and the other disciples in a room to have a last meal together. [Pause] Look around you. Some of the other disciples are celebrating; they don't know what is going on. [Pause] It is evening, and the room is dark. Smell the good smells of the food. [Pause] As you hear the story read, continue to imagine that you are Peter. Live out the story."

The story of Jesus washing the disciples' feet (John 13:1–17) is read slowly, with significant pauses between sentences.

"Now take a moment and speak to Jesus about what he has just done for you."

The students remain silent for another minute. The teacher ends the exercise by debriefing, including this question: "What does Jesus ask of his followers?"

A Variation: If you think your group of kids is serious enough to do so without silliness, ask them to wash one another's hands with a bowl of water and a fluffy towel. It can be done in an atmosphere of prayer and reverence, and afterward students can share their feelings about washing the hands of another, and having their own hands washed.

Another Variation: Tie this meditation exercise in with the ritual washing of feet which is done at most parishes on Holy Thursday. Perhaps some students could be special helpers or attendants at this Holy Thursday Mass, or they could meet shortly afterward to have a special prayer time about what they just participated in.

A Good Catch
(Luke 5:1–11)

Have the students tune in.

"Imagine that you are a fisherman named Andrew. You and your brother, Simon, run a fishing business. [Pause] You fish at night or in the early morning, and you have just spent hours and hours fishing, but have caught nothing at all. [Pause] You are dead tired. Your back and arms ache from rowing and pulling in nets. [Pause] As you pull in to shore, a strange man, followed by a crowd, arrives at the edge of the water. As you hear the rest of the story, continue to imagine that you are really there."

The call of the first disciples (Luke 5:1–11) is read slowly, with significant pauses between sentences.

"Say something now to God about what it feels like to be called by name to be a follower of Jesus."

The students remain silent for another minute. The teacher ends the exercise by debriefing, including these questions:

- Do you think Jesus still calls people by name to be his followers?
- Do you think he calls women, too?
- Do you feel called by Jesus?
- Whom do you know of that you think is called by Jesus?
- Is it possible that everybody is called to be a follower of Jesus?
- The story says that Andrew and Peter left everything behind to follow Jesus. What do you think you would have to leave behind to follow him?

Get Up and Walk!
(Luke 5:17–26)

Have the students tune in.

"Pretend that you are a woman living in a little village near the Sea of Galilee. One day Jesus comes to your house with a whole crowd of people. [Pause] They jam into your little house. There are people everywhere, friends and strangers. They sit and stand all around. [Pause] Jesus is telling stories and teaching about God. You listen eagerly; he is really interesting, and funny, too. [Pause] As you listen to the rest of the story, pretend that the events are really happening right now. See and hear them taking place."

The healing of a paralyzed man (Luke 5:17–26) is read slowly with significant pauses between sentences.

"Now pretend that you are sitting right next to Jesus. Say something to him about what he just did in your house."

The students remain silent for another minute. The teacher ends the exercise by debriefing, including these questions:

- Is it more important to have your sins forgiven, or to be healed physically?
- What is the connection between sickness and sin?
- Was the man paralyzed because he was a sinner?

Season's Greetings from Jesus
(John 10:10)

This is a good meditation exercise to use with the kids just before their Christmas holidays. The kids will need a pencil and paper to use as part of their prayer. It will be helpful to have some peaceful background music to play while the kids do their writing.

Have the students tune in.

"It is almost Christmas now. Maybe you wonder why Jesus was born. [Pause] Listen to these words of Jesus and he will tell you why he came: 'I came so that you could have life, life in all its fullness' [John 10:10]. [Pause] 'I came so that you could have life, life in all its fullness.' Write on your paper what these words mean to you."

The students remain silent and work for another three minutes or so. The teacher ends the exercise by debriefing.

A Variation: Instead of having the kids write what the words of Jesus mean to them, suggest that they write a note to Jesus about his words. They might need a little more time for this.

This Is My Body

The students need a pencil and a piece of paper for this exercise. Have the students tune in.

"Listen carefully to these words: On the night he was betrayed, Jesus took bread. He broke the bread, gave it to his disciples, and said, 'Take this, all of you, and eat it; this is my body, which will be given up for you.' After the supper he took a cup filled with wine. Again he gave God thanks and praise and said, 'This is the cup of my blood, the blood of the new and everlasting covenant. It will be shed for you and for all people so that sin may be forgiven. Do this in memory of me.'

"On your piece of paper, write a note to God about those words."

The students work on this for two or three minutes. The teacher ends the exercise by debriefing.

One of You Will Betray Me
(John 13:21–30)

Have the students tune in.

"Imagine that you are one of Jesus' disciples. You are at the Last Supper with him. It is the night before he will die. [Pause] There is plenty of lamb, crispy unleavened bread, and other good food to eat. There is lots of good wine to drink. Everyone is having a good time. [Pause] Jesus is looking upset or worried over something. You are not sure why. [Pause] As you hear the story, pretend that you are really there and that the events are actually happening."

John 13:21–30 is read slowly, with significant pauses between the sentences.

"It is night. There is darkness all around. How do you feel? [Pause] Take a moment and speak to God about that."

The students remain silent for another minute. The teacher ends the exercise by debriefing.

In the Garden of Gethsemane
(Luke 22:40–44)

Have the students tune in.

"Imagine that you are a close friend of Jesus. Maybe you are one of the twelve apostles. Maybe you are some other close friend. [Pause] You have just finished the Last Supper with Jesus. The two of you leave the dining room and walk to a pretty garden. It is night. [Pause] The air is cool. There is a nice breeze, and far away you can hear the sounds of the city. [Pause] Tomorrow Jesus will be killed. As you hear this story from Luke's Gospel, pretend that you are really there."

Luke 22:40–44 (Jesus prays in the garden of Gethsemane) is read very slowly, with significant pauses between sentences.

"What would you say to Jesus?"

The students remain silent for another two minutes. The teacher ends the exercise by debriefing.

Arrest Him!
(John 18:1–13)

Have the students tune in.

"Imagine that you are a soldier in Jerusalem. You live in a barrack with a lot of other soldiers. [Pause] You have armor and a helmet made of leather, which is very hot to wear. You have a big, heavy sword to carry. [Pause] Usually life is pretty boring. You are just a guard. This night your commander comes in to get you and some of the other soldiers. You have a special job to do. [Pause] You put on your leather armor and get your sword. You are going to arrest a man named Jesus. [Pause] You don't know much about him. You have heard that he is a religious nut or something. You wonder what he is really like. Some of the things he has said sound pretty good. [Pause] You get in line and set off for a garden to arrest Jesus. [Pause] As you hear the rest of the story, pretend that you are really there, and that it is actually happening to you."

The arrest of Jesus (John 18:1–13) is read slowly, with significant pauses between the sentences.

"How do you feel about arresting Jesus? Explain your feelings to God."

The students remain silent for another minute. The teacher ends the exercise by debriefing.

A Variation: After reading the passage from John, have the students imagine that they have some time at Annas' house to talk with Jesus and to ask him questions. Have them imagine that conversation.

Another Variation: After imagining the conversation in the first variation, have the students write out a dialogue between the soldier and Jesus. One or more such dialogues could even be acted out.

Peace Be with You!
(John 24:36–53)

Have the students tune in.

"Pretend that you are one of the original twelve apostles. It is just a couple of days after Jesus was killed. The remaining eleven apostles, you included, are hidden in an attic room, scared to go out. Everyone is frightened because they might be killed, too. [Pause] Two of the disciples have just come in all excited and breathless. They have some wild story about seeing Jesus while walking down the road. They are excited, but you think they are crazy. [Pause] Listen to what happened next. As you hear the story, imagine that it is really happening."

John 24:36–53 is read, with significant pauses between the sentences.

"Now speak to God about what that must have been like."

The students remain silent for another minute. The teacher ends the exercise by debriefing.

On the Road to Emmaus
(Luke 24:13–35)

Have the students tune in.

"Imagine that you are together with a friend, walking down a road from Jerusalem to a little town called Emmaus. The road is hot and dusty. You are tired. [Pause] You and your friend were friends of Jesus, who was killed a couple of days ago. You feel terrible about that. You feel frightened and very sad. [Pause] As you walk, you talk quietly about your friend Jesus. You feel like crying. [Pause] As you listen to the rest of the story, pretend that it is actually happening to you and your friend."

Luke 24:13–35 is read slowly, with significant pauses between sentences.

"Take a moment now to pretend that you have to explain to the other disciples what has just happened. Imagine what you would actually say to them."

The students remain silent for another minute. The teacher ends the exercise by debriefing, including these questions:

- How did the disciples recognize Jesus?
- How can we recognize Jesus?
- Jesus said, "Do this in memory of me." What was he talking about? Is that what this story is about?

Symbols and Prayer

Symbols can communicate meaning to people in very powerful ways. They are like words or concepts made visible and tangible. They are memorable: any good teacher knows that students remember more about something if they see and touch it, instead of merely hearing about it. Furthermore, a good symbol does not need to be explained. It speaks for itself, and much more powerfully than any words could. For instance, one cannot describe light; one must experience light, and it will be an experience never to be forgotten.

Symbols are powerful aids to prayer. Our liturgies and sacramental rites are filled with symbols, and that is what makes them so powerful, so interesting, and so unforgettable. Even outside of the context of ritual, symbols can be used to help people pray more deeply and intently. The following exercises make use of symbols in an attempt to help middle school kids to pray.

Fire and Light

This works best in a darkened room. Have the students sit in a circle. Light a candle and place it on the floor in the middle of the circle. It is important to use a candle whose flame will be easily visible to everyone.

Have the students tune in.

"Open your eyes now, and look into the flame of the candle. Concentrate on the flame as it leaps and changes its color and shape. Block out everything else. [Pause for one minute.] Look around the room a bit. You can see that things close to the candle are visible; things far away are not. [Pause] Light from the candle shows us the world around us. It lets us see things as they truly are. If you were lost, light could help you find your way back. [Pause] Go back to concentrating on the flame. The flame is warm. Warmth keeps us alive. It makes plants grow in the spring. Warmth can be used to cook food, or to make things. Fire gives light and warmth. [Pause]

"Jesus said, 'I am the light of the world.' Jesus guides us and shows us reality just like the light from this flame. [Pause] John's Gospel tells us that Jesus is a light which shines on the world, a light which will never, ever go out. [Pause]

"Look at the top of the candle. The wax melts and is drawn into the flame. The wax makes the flame bigger and brighter. [Pause] Jesus also said, 'You are the light of the world.' When we let ourselves be drawn into his flame, we make it brighter. We burn with Jesus and we help to give light to the world. [Pause] Look deeply into the flame. We are the flame; the flame is us. You are the light of Christ. Become the flame."

The students remain silent for another minute. The teacher ends the exercise by debriefing, including this question: How can each person help the light of Christ to shine on the world?

A Variation: At night, take the kids outdoors and build a wood fire. Have them sit in a circle around the fire for the exercise.

Water

For this exercise each student will need a small cup of water. A clear cup would be preferable. These should be given to each student before they center themselves.

Have the students tune in.

"Open your eyes now and look into your cup of water. See only the water; block out everything else. [Pause] See how clean the water is. See how pure it is. [Pause] Move the water around by tilting your cup. See it flow and move. [Pause] Close your eyes again. Touch the water to your lips, but do not drink any. [Pause] Hold the water to your lips and continue to feel it. Feel the softness. Feel the cool. [Pause] Drink some of your water very slowly. Roll it gently in your mouth and let it trickle down your throat. [Pause] Drink as much as you want. [Pause] Water is refreshing; when you are tired it helps make you feel better. [Pause] Water gives life. Without it you would die. [Pause]

"Jesus said, 'Come to me, all you who are weary and find life burdensome, and I will give you rest.' [Pause] Jesus once said, 'I can give you life-giving water. Whoever drinks water from a well will get thirsty again, but whoever drinks the water that I will give will never be thirsty again. The water that I will give becomes a spring in the person which will give him life-giving water and also eternal life.' [Pause] Take a minute now and thank God for the gift of life."

The students remain silent for another minute. The teacher ends the exercise by debriefing.

Manger

For this exercise a manger from a Christmas nativity set is needed. The manger should be big enough to hold a real baby, if possible, and be filled with straw. It is placed in the middle of a circle of students.

Have the students tune in.

"Open your eyes and look closely at the manger. Try to see every possible detail. Try to block out everything else. [Pause for one minute.] There were some shepherds in the nearby fields watching over their flocks of sheep. An angel of the Lord appeared to them, and God's glory shone all around them. [Pause] They were terribly afraid, but the angel said, 'Don't be afraid! I am here to bring you good news, which will be a joy for all people. Today a Savior was born in the city of David: Christ the Lord. This will be your sign: you will find a baby wrapped in swaddling clothes and lying in a manger.' [Pause]

"Imagine what it was like for Jesus to spend the first night of his life lying in that manger. [Pause] Take a minute now and speak to Jesus about that."

The students remain silent for another minute. The teacher ends the exercise by debriefing.

Forever and Ever

For this meditation exercise the teacher must prepare a poster board with a large plain circle drawn on it. The circle's line should be thick, sharp, and perfectly round. The poster is placed on the floor in the middle of the circle of students.

Have the students tune in.

"Look at the circle now. Stare at it deeply, and block out everything else. [Pause] Now focus on one place on the circle. [Pause] Slowly move your eyes so that they move around the circle. Keep on going around the circle, slowly, slowly. [Pause for one minute.] A circle has no end. It doesn't even have a beginning. It just keeps on going and going, forever and ever and ever. [Pause] God is like a circle. He was never born and he will never die. He always was and always will be. [Pause] God is forever. God is eternal. [Pause] Take a minute now and say something to God about his eternity."

The students remain silent for another minute. The teacher ends the exercise by debriefing.

A Variation: Instead of using a poster with a circle drawn on it, place an electric train or electric car on a circular track in the midst of the students. Have the students focus on the train or car as it goes around.

Oil

Oil is an important symbol for several of our sacraments: baptism, confirmation, anointing of the sick, and holy orders. This exercise helps the students to have a meaningful experience of oil. It would work especially well following instruction on one or more of the above sacraments.

A dish of salad oil or baby oil is needed (salad oil or olive oil is best, because that is what is used for the sacraments). The dish should be clear glass so that the oil is visible. Do not fill the dish or the oil will be spilled as the students pass it around. Place the dish of oil in the circle of students where all can see, but within your own reach.

Have the students tune in.

"Open your eyes now and look at the oil. Focus in on it, and try to block out everything else. [Pause for one minute.] Pass the dish around carefully. Each person should dip one finger in the oil. Catch any drips in the palm of the other hand. Do not wipe off the oil. [Wait for all to get some oil.] Now close your eyes.

72

Rub the oil between your fingers and thumb. Feel its smoothness. [Pause] Now slowly begin to rub the oil into your hands. Rub it all around, smoothly and slowly. [Pause] Feel the softness of the oil. Feel it sink into your skin. [Pause] Some of the oil has sunk into your skin. It has become part of you. It will not wash off. [Pause] God is like oil. He sinks into us deeply. He will never leave us."

The students remain silent for another minute. The teacher ends the exercise by debriefing.

Wind and Spirit

For this exercise a sound recording of the wind blowing is needed. It should be at least ten minutes long. It will be even better if the wind noises vary: sometimes loud, sometimes soft.

Have the students tune in.

"Listen now for three or four minutes to the sound of the wind. Let the sounds right into your heart. Feel the wind. Become the wind. [Pause for three or four minutes while the recording of the wind plays. Then reduce the volume sufficiently so that the students may easily hear you speak.] The Holy Spirit is like the wind. It blows wherever it wants to and whenever it wants to. [Pause] Sometimes the Holy Spirit blows softly. Sometimes it blows very strongly. [Pause] You can't see the Holy Spirit, just as you cannot see the wind. You can only see what they do. Listen to the wind."

The volume of the recording is turned up again. After about four more minutes of play, the teacher ends the exercise by slowly turning down the volume, pausing, and then debriefing the students. The teacher asks:

- How can you tell when the Holy Spirit is blowing on the world?
- How can you tell when the Holy Spirit is working in your life?
- Are there any times that you have seen the Holy Spirit "blow" you around?

Pain

It may seem crazy when you first hear of it, but the experience of pain often brings people closer to God. Suffering can be a deeply scriptural experience. Our Christian theology has always affirmed this: through suffering we are able to conform ourselves to Christ, to share in his paschal mystery of death and resurrection. Middle school kids have learned all of their lives how to avoid pain. It will not occur to many of them that the experience of pain can also be enlightening.

Clyde Reid, in his little book, *Celebrate the Temporary*, provides a marvelous meditation on pain (New York: Harper & Row, pages 43–56). I wish that I had thought of it! Get hold of his book and try the exercise he suggests with middle school kids.

Caution: I am not suggesting that you teach the kids to "mortify their flesh" or inflict pain upon themselves. Rather, the above exercise helps them to come to a deeper understanding of the pain which is inevitably a part of human life.

When you debrief the kids after the exercise, include the following questions:

- What were times when you felt a lot of pain?
- Does pain cause you to turn to God?
- Are you afraid of pain?
- Can you learn from pain?
- Do you think suffering brings people closer to God, or drives them away from him?

Time Runs Out

For this exercise an hour glass is needed. It would be best to have an hour glass at least six inches tall, and whose sand runs completely through in about five minutes. Place the hour glass in the center of the group of students. Have the students tune in. Turn the hour glass over so that the sand starts to run through.

"Look at the hour glass. Block out everything else. [Pause] See the sand pour through. It never speeds up or slows down. It just keeps going. [Pause] Each person has a limited amount of time to live. Some people have lots of time; some people have a little time. But sooner or later, everyone's sand runs out. [Pause] Watch the sand. Think about your life. One day it will end. [The students remain silent until all the sand runs through, unless this would take too long.] Now close your eyes, and say something to Jesus about your time and your life."

The students remain silent for another minute. The teacher ends the exercise by debriefing.

Take and Eat . . . Take and Drink

For this exercise a large, attractive piece of bread and a goblet of wine are needed. The bread should be plain and without decorations. The wine should be reddish in color, and should be placed in a clear goblet so that it may be seen. The bread and wine are placed in the center of the group of students.

Have the students tune in.

"Open your eyes now and look at the bread and wine. Block out all other sights. [Pause] See the color of the wine. Imagine how it smells and tastes; maybe you can actually smell it. [Pause] See the bread's color and texture. Imagine how the bread feels and tastes. [Pause] While you continue to look at the bread and wine, listen to these words:

"The night before he died, Jesus took a piece of bread. He broke the bread, gave it to his disciples, and said, 'Take this, all of you, and eat it; this is my body, which will be given up for you.' [Pause for one minute.] After the supper Jesus took a cup filled with wine. Again he gave God thanks and praise and said, 'This is the cup of my blood, the blood of the new and everlasting covenant. It will be shed for you and for all people so that sin may be forgiven. Do this in memory of me.' [Pause] As you continue to look at the bread and wine, think about those words and actions of Jesus."

The students remain silent for another minute. The teacher ends the exercise by debriefing.

As Big as the Sky

This is a good exercise to do with the students on one of those beautiful spring days when it is hard to stay indoors. Take the students outside to some quiet location and have them begin to look up at the sky. They will probably do best if they lie down on the ground. (Make sure that no one is looking up at the sun—you don't want any damaged eyes!) After the students get settled and quiet, ask them to tune in, but remaining in whatever posture they find comfortable for sky-gazing.

"Look up into the sky now. See the blue. Look into it deeply and try to see the bottom of the blue. [Pause] Look at the clouds. Try to see if any of them are moving, even very slightly. [Pause for one minute] You are looking at hundreds, maybe thousands, of miles of sky. Picture yourself way, way up there. Imagine how tiny you would be in that big sky. [Pause] God is bigger than the sky. God is bigger than a million skies, or hundreds of millions. [Pause] Imagine how big God is and how tiny you are. Say something to God about that."

The students remain silent for another minute, or longer if they are still and quiet. The teacher ends the exercise by debriefing.

A Variation: Instead of taking the students out of doors, use slide images of clouds and sky.

Long, Long Ago, in a Galaxy Far, Far Away . . .

This is a wonderful exercise to use with the students on a starry night. Take them outdoors and find a place where they may look up at the stars. If it is too cold to lie or sit on the ground, they might need chairs, although this should be avoided if at all possible; lying on the ground works best. Have the students get comfortable and begin looking up at the stars. After they are quiet and settled, have them tune in, but remaining in whatever posture they find comfortable for star-gazing.

"Open your eyes now and look at the stars. See how many you can count. [Pause for one minute.] Notice how the stars flicker. See how some are brighter than others. [Pause] Pick out your favorite star. Pick one that will be special just for you. [Pause for one minute.] Many of the stars you can see are hundreds of millions of light years away. That means that the light rays that are entering your eyes now left those stars hundreds of millions of years ago. [Pause] Maybe your favorite star blew up and disappeared ten million years ago, and we just don't know it yet. We might not know it for another ten million years. [Pause] If each star had nine or ten planets going around it like our sun, imagine how many planets that would be. Imagine how many worlds could be out there; maybe some have people like us. [Pause] The world God made is so huge and so old. But God is even bigger and older. Take a moment now and speak to God about that."

The students remain silent for another minute, or even longer if they remain quiet and intent. The teacher ends the exercise by debriefing.

You Have Called Us Out of Darkness

For this exercise a completely dark room is required. This exercise has tremendous impact on the students, but only if the darkness is total. Any room with a window cannot be used; some light will seep in. When you think you have found a room which is sufficiently dark, stay there for fifteen or twenty minutes. If you are able to see objects or shapes in the room at all, it is not sufficiently dark.

76

Bring the students into the dark room (using some light to guide them) and get them settled in their meditation postures. Douse the lights, and have them tune in.

"It is very rare to experience total darkness. It is like nothing you have ever experienced before. [Pause] Open your eyes. See the blackness all around you. [Pause] Feel the darkness. If you try, you can actually feel it. [Pause] What feelings do you have inside yourself now? [Pause] Fear? [Pause] Anxiety? [Pause] Imagine for a moment that you are trapped in this darkness. Imagine that you can never get out. [Pause] Jesus promised that he would be the light of the world. [Pause] Take a moment now to tell God how it feels to be in the dark. Ask him to be your light."

The students remain silent for another minute. The teacher ends the exercise by turning on the lights and debriefing.

Note: Obviously, to make this work, the teacher must memorize the directions which are given to the students.

The Praying Hands

Hands are a powerful symbol. In the Old and New Testaments the laying on of hands was a powerful sign of God's presence: in choosing a king or prophet, in healing the sick or crippled, in the gift of the Holy Spirit, in the choosing of ministers. The laying on of hands is part of the rituals of confirmation, reconciliation, anointing of the sick, and holy orders. This meditation helps the kids focus in a rudimentary way upon hands as a symbol.

If possible, the students should sit so as not to face each other. Have the students tune in.

"Hold your hands in front of you in your lap. Keep your eyes closed and imagine what your hands must look like. [Pause] Notice how your hands feel. Feel their strength. [Pause] Open your hands and hold them as if you are waiting for someone to put something into them. Imagine how they look. [Pause] Open your eyes and look at your hands. Try to block out any other sight. [Pause] Now imagine Jesus putting a gift into your hands. [Pause] Close your eyes and thank Jesus for his gift."

The students remain silent for another minute. The teacher ends the exercise by debriefing.

The Old Rugged Cross

Have the students tune in.

"Imagine that you are seated on a rocky hilltop. You are all alone. [Pause] In front of you is a big wooden cross. It stands ten feet high. [Pause] The wood of the cross is very rough. There are lots of splinters sticking out. The color is a light tan. The wood looks very hard. [Pause] There are three holes in the cross: two are near the ends of the crossbeam and one is on the vertical piece about four feet up from the ground. They are nail holes. [Pause] Concentrate on the cross now. Concentrate on its shape, its color, and the look of the wood. If your mind wanders, keep coming back to look at the cross."

The students remain silent for three minutes. The teacher ends the exercise by debriefing.

Crown of Thorns

Have the students tune in.

"Imagine that you are standing in the middle of a desert. It is very hot and dry. [Pause] You look around and on the ground a few feet away you see a crown of thorns. [Pause] It is a long branch woven around several times in a circle. The thorns are two inches long and as sharp as needles. [Pause] Concentrate on the crown of thorns. When your mind wanders, come back to it. [Pause for three minutes.] Now take a minute to speak to God about that."

The students remain silent for another minute. The teacher ends the exercise by debriefing.

More Mantras

Most of the prayer exercises suggested in this book are heavily laden with content: they invite the kids to recall, to imagine, to fantasize, to see, to hear, and to express themselves in various ways. Such prayer forms are often placed in a category called "meditation."

But at another, and some say higher, level is a form of prayer which has as little content as possible: this is often called "contemplation." The popularity of contemplation in Christian spirituality may be traced back at least to a medieval book called *The Cloud of Unknowing*, written by an anonymous English author. Thomas Merton, a great Roman Catholic mystic of the twentieth century, called this type of prayer "centering prayer," a label which has become popular.

Contemplation, or centering prayer, involves settling into oneself as deeply as possible. In finding the center of one's own being, one can experience God's presence in a more direct or mystical way. Rather than thinking many intense thoughts, the goal is to empty the mind of any thought. In so doing, one becomes open to God's presence.

The beginning of centering prayer is what I have called "tuning in." As deep breathing is established, the person begins to repeat over and over a prayer formula, sometimes called a "mantra." Repeating such a formula over and over helps to empty the mind of the many thoughts and preoccupations which usually distract a person.

For the most part, middle school kids will not find contemplation to be very helpful or important. They will not be able to sustain such inner concentration long enough. At the same time, "tuning in" does help them to quiet down and become ready for meditation, which has enough content to keep them interested.

Encourage your students to practice the tuning in techniques as they are outlined in the Introduction. Invite them to make use of some of the following mantras. Each formula has two parts: one part to be thought during each inhalation, and a second part to be thought during each exhalation. The same mantra should be used for any single prayer time. The kids may find it interesting to have a list from which to choose, and they should be encouraged to choose a mantra which relates to their prayer needs at the present time. For example, if a student feels troubled over a problem, he might select "Jesus—Peace."

Some students may find centering prayer to be rewarding and useful in itself, rather than merely as a prelude to the more meditative prayer forms suggested in this book. Such interest should be encouraged. Many great mystics and spiritual writers assert that contemplative prayer is the highest form of all.

The "Jesus Prayer"
One of the most popular mantras is often called the "Jesus Prayer." It is a good place to start with the kids. It involves cycles of two inhalations and exhalations.

Inhale	**Exhale**
Lord Jesus Christ . . .	Son of God
Have mercy on me . . .	A sinner.

Other suggested mantras are:

Inhale	Exhale
Lord Jesus Christ . . .	Touch my heart
	Come to me
or	Be with me
God my Father . . .	Give me peace
	Heal my soul
or	Lift me up
Holy Spirit . . .	Hold me close
	Take my hand
	Hear my prayer
	Walk with me
	Stay with me
	Abide with me
	Teach me truth
	Give me faith
	Show me love
	Be my hope
	Light my way
Lord Jesus Christ . . .	Son of David
	Lamb of God
	Prince of Peace
	King of Kings
	Son of God
	Son of Man
	Lord of Life
	Word of God
	Lord of Lords
	Light of the World
Lord Jesus . . .	Heal me
	Touch me
	Fill me
	Hold me
	Console me
	Hear me
	Love me
	Teach me
Jesus . . .	Come
	Lord
	Mercy
	Brother
	Power
	Strength

Praying for Others

Praying for others is a central and essential aspect of Christian spirituality. Jesus himself often prayed for others, and his example is one that we should follow. These exercises are designed to help the kids to pray for others in deeper and more meaningful ways. They provide a rich resource for discussion and learning about prayer and faith. For example, the teacher should be prepared to spend time on questions such as the following:

- Does it matter when we pray for other people? Does it really help?
- Does God listen to our prayers for other people more than he listens to prayers for ourselves?
- If God knew what to do to help a person, wouldn't he just do it anyway, whether we prayed or not?
- We prayed for a sick person, and he died anyway. What good did we do? Didn't God listen to us?

These questions and others like them will come up if some of the following exercises are used. Questions concerning the effectiveness of prayer for others are difficult to answer. The teacher should not try to provide quick and easy answers to questions like the ones listed above; rather, the students should be helped to struggle with these questions and to find their own answers. I still struggle with most of them myself, but for me the bottom line is this: Jesus prayed for others as well as trying to help them in other ways; he is our example to follow, even when we don't completely understand.

The Lord Be with You!

Have the students tune in.

"Think of your favorite school friends. As you think of each one, picture him or her. You might even imagine yourself saying hello and getting an answer back from your friend. [Pause for one minute.] Now go through your list of friends again. This time, as you picture each one, ask God to be with him or her. Ask God to give each friend his protection. [Pause for one minute.] Go through your list of friends a third time. As you picture each one, thank God for giving you that friend."

The students remain silent for another minute. The teacher ends the exercise by debriefing.

Way To Go!

Have the students tune in.

"Think of a friend or family member who has recently accomplished something good. [Pause] Maybe your friend got a good grade on a hard test, or did well in a sporting event, or finished an important project, or won some kind of award. [Pause] Imagine your friend accomplishing whatever it was. Picture it in your mind as if you were watching it on television. [Pause for one minute.] Now take a minute and thank God for helping your friend and allowing him or her to accomplish that good thing."

The students remain silent for another minute. The teacher ends the exercise by debriefing.

Parents and Others

Have the students tune in.

"Think of your parents, or whomever you live with who takes care of you each day. [Pause] Imagine that they are sitting there, right in front of you. [Pause] How do they look? What are they wearing? [Pause] What is their mood? Are they happy, sad, alert, tired, or what? [Pause] Look deeply into their eyes. Try to feel how they are feeling. [Pause] Take a minute now and ask God to be with your parents (or whoever it is). Ask God to help them to be good parents, and to help them to raise you well."

The students remain silent for another minute. The teacher ends the exercise by debriefing.

Variations: Do this same exercise focusing on other important individuals in the kids' lives: teachers, coaches, doctors, etc.

For Those Who Can't Be with Us

Frequently in a classroom situation one or more members of the class will be absent. This exercise provides a way to pray for those who cannot be with the class at a particular time. It is a beautiful custom to pray for absent members of a classroom community. When this is done habitually, those who are absent will know that they are being prayed for. This knowledge truly will strengthen the bonds of friendship among the students. This exercise can be a daily (or weekly) event.

The teacher should prepare the kids for this exercise by noting with them who is absent that day. If possible, the reasons for the classmates' absence should be mentioned: e.g., sickness, travel, family crisis, etc. Then the teacher should have the students tune in.

"We pray now for our friends. As each friend's name is mentioned, picture him or her before you. Ask God to be with that friend and to bring him or her safely back to our class."

The names of absent students are mentioned, with a pause of about thirty seconds after each name. After all are mentioned, the teacher ends the exercise by debriefing.

A Variation: Have the students compose a generic sort of prayer asking God to be with absent friends. It should be fairly short and easily memorized. At the completion of the above exercise, the prayer is recited by the group in unison. This practice can easily become a regular ritual for the class.

Here's My Friend, God!

Have the students tune in.

"Imagine a friend of yours who needs help with some kind of problem. Picture the friend and what he or she needs. [Pause] Now tell God about that friend and his or her need. Ask God to help. [Pause] Imagine yourself helping that person to solve the problem."

The students remain silent for another minute. The teacher ends the exercise by debriefing. These questions should be posed to the students:

- When we pray for God's help, what responsibility do we have to do something?
- You imagined how you could help your friend. Was that something that you could *really* do? Would you like to actually help your friend?

Sad Friend

Have the students tune in.

"Think of a sad event that happened to someone you love or to someone that you know very well. [Pause] How long ago did this happen? Do you think your friend still feels sad? [Pause] If you can, replay the event as if you were watching it on television. If you didn't actually see it, imagine how it must have happened. [Pause for one minute.] Now tell God about that sad event and your friend."

The students remain silent for another two minutes. The teacher ends the exercise by debriefing.

Mass Intentions

It is always important for Christians to situate their prayer lives within the context of a believing community. Catholics usually do this by means of liturgy and other public worship. This exercise will help the students to connect themselves in a new way with the prayer life of their parish community.

Explain to the students that Mass intentions are the Church's way of praying for special causes, especially for those who have died. Each Mass in a parish is offered with a special need, person, or intention in mind. Even though unable to attend all of those Masses, the students can join in the prayer effort by remembering those same intentions in their private or classroom prayer.

After the students have tuned in, the teacher simply announces the name of the person for whom that day's parish Mass is being offered (or whatever the intention is). The students are asked to take a brief moment and ask God to be with that person. If this is a daily exercise, it is probably not necessary to debrief the students most of the time.

Mass intentions may usually be found in the parish bulletin or obtained from the parish office.

A Variation: In addition to the above exercise, have the students send a note or card to the family of the deceased person, assuring them of the class' prayers.

For Our Sick

This exercise helps the students to pray for fellow parishioners who are sick or homebound for reasons of age or health. The teacher should obtain from the pastor or parish office a list of such people.

Have the students tune in.

"Here is a list of our fellow parishioners who are sick. Some are in the hospital or nursing home, and some are stuck at home. Some will probably recover from their illness, and others will probably die. [Pause] As you hear each person's name, ask God to be with him or her. Ask God to heal the person, if that is his will."

The names of the sick are read one at a time, with a pause of about thirty seconds after each name. After the last name has been read, the teacher ends the exercise by debriefing.

Caution: Don't try to use more than six or eight names. The kids will not be able to focus that long. If there are more sick people than that, divide the list into groups of six and use the various groups on different days.

A Variation: Have each student make a get-well card for a sick person in the parish. Have the students sit in a circle, holding their cards, and center themselves. Place a basket or box in the center of the circle. After all are quiet, let each student place his or her card in the basket, announcing the name of the sick person to whom the card will be sent. Invite the students to be praying for the sick as their names are mentioned.

Suggestion Box

This exercise will help your class to deepen their sense of worth and importance as praying Christians. Have the kids make a prayer request box and place it in some public location in the school or church. Let the other classes (or the parishioners) know that prayer requests may be placed in the box, and that your class will pray for those intentions. On a regular basis (daily, weekly, monthly, etc.) remove any prayer requests in the box and screen them (some will be frivolous or sarcastic).

Have the students tune in. When all are quiet, read each prayer request and pause for thirty seconds or so to let the kids pray silently. Conclude with a group prayer such as the Our Father.

Before too long, your class will have a reputation as helpful and caring "prayers." This is an excellent teaching and formation opportunity.

Adopt a Patient

This exercise helps the entire class to focus its spiritual energy on praying for one special person. Each week or month, the class can "adopt" a patient at a nearby hospital. Whenever the class prays together, they can take a brief moment to pray for that patient. This will work especially well if the students can be given periodic updates on the patient's condition.

Logistically, the teacher needs a good contact at the hospital. I suggest the hospital chaplain. In order to protect the privacy of the patient, the teacher might give him or her a fictitious first name. When the patient's medical crisis is over (either because of recovery or death) the class can begin to pray for a new patient.

A Variation: Tell the kids who the patient really is, and invite them to make individual cards, or a class card, for the patient or the patient's family. In the card they could express their sympathy and promise to pray for the patient. The cards can be incorporated into group prayer: see the Variation in "For Our Sick."

For the World

This exercise helps the students to pray for other people in "the world out there," people they have never met or possibly even heard of before. The teacher or student selects from the day's newspaper a story about people somewhere in the world who need help. They might be victims of natural disaster, people living in war zones, sick people, starving people, etc. The teacher needs to select an excerpt from the news story which gives the essential information, but which can be read aloud in one minute or less.

Have the students tune in.

"Here is a story about people who need God's help. Listen carefully to the story. Imagine what it must be like to be these people (or this person). [The excerpt from the news story is slowly read.] Take a minute now and ask God to help these people."

The students remain silent for another minute. The teacher ends the exercise by debriefing.

Multi-Media Meditations

Photographic slides can be tremendously effective in helping middle school kids to focus their concentration and thus to pray better. Our contemporary American culture has conditioned the kids to relate to visual images on a screen: most middle school kids spend several hours a day watching television. Through long years of practice, they have learned to stare intently at virtually any illuminated screen. This capacity can be exploited to help the kids to pray.

The most effective way to use photographic slides is to project them while appropriate music is played. This greatly increases their impact (and it increases the impact of the music, which might itself be an aid to prayer). This section contains some examples of effective slide and music shows. It is far more exciting to create your own, and the slide and music shows suggested here are simply examples which set the pattern to follow.

How To Make a Slide and Music Show for Prayer

The slide and music show must have a clear and straightforward message to convey, a message which helps the students to reflect and pray. The message could be that God has created a marvelously beautiful world, that there are many people who suffer, that God's people offer him praise and thanksgiving, etc. But it must be clear.

Slides may be found to match a particular piece of music, or vice versa. It really doesn't matter which is chosen first, as long as they go together.

Many publishing houses offer packages of slides for sale which are excellent for the purpose of aiding prayer. Often these slide packages are designed to be "message-laden," and they seek to depict important spiritual or religious themes. Ambitious catechists can take their own slides. This is especially exciting, if also time-consuming. The slides must be of good quality, or they will detract from rather than enhance the meditation experience.

To sort and arrange slides in a good order, it is helpful to have an illuminated board on which to place them. These are available at moderate cost at any good camera store or department.

Generally, when slides are set to music, each should be projected for five to ten seconds. Shorter periods for each slide produce a flashy effect; longer periods make the show boring.

The slides may be matched to the words of a song, or may be changed at regular intervals, e.g., every five seconds, if the music has no words. In either case, the show should be rehearsed several times before it is used with the kids in order to make sure that the timing is precise and correct. If you are particularly lucky, your library or resource center will have a cassette recorder and slide projector system which allows inaudible signals to be recorded on the music tape: the signals tell the projector automatically when to change the slides.

If you like to be creative, produce your own sight and sound shows, or let the students make their own. The result is well worth the effort.

Sunset

The teacher must obtain a slide of a beautiful sunset.

Have the students tune in. Project the slide onto the screen when all are quiet and settled.

"Open your eyes now and look at the sunset. [Pause] Some people are reminded of death when they see a sunset. Other people think romantic thoughts about love. [Pause] Maybe the sunset makes you think of something else. [Pause] How does it make you feel? What mood does it put you in? [Pause] Look deeply into the sunset. See the oranges, the yellows, the reds. Become the colors. [Pause] Take a couple of minutes to continue looking, and tell God how you feel."

The students remain silent for another two minutes. The teacher ends the exercise by debriefing.

Creation

This exercise is designed to help the students appreciate the beauty and goodness of God's creation. The teacher must obtain forty or fifty slides depicting a sunrise and other beautiful nature scenes. These are shown, accompanied by the Cat Stevens song, "Morning Has Broken" (on the album *Teaser and the Firecat* [Hollywood: A & M Records]).

Have the students tune in.

"This is a beautiful song with beautiful pictures. Just take it easy and enjoy it. Let it sink in."

The music and slide show is played.

"Now take a minute to thank God for making such a beautiful world for you to live in."

The students remain silent for another minute. The teacher ends the exercise by debriefing.

"Where Do the Children Play?"

This meditation experience is designed to foster the kids' awareness of threats to the environment. It would be particularly effective following a presentation on creation theology (the goodness of God's creation, our stewardship over the goods of the earth, etc.). A fitting response to this experience would be some action on behalf of environmental protection.

The teacher must obtain forty to fifty slides which show various ways in which our natural environment is hurt or destroyed. It is easy to take the slides yourself, since appropriate subject matter is all around. It can be done in the city or country. The slides are shown, accompanied by the Cat Stevens song, "Where Do the Children Play?" (on the album *Tea for the Tillerman* [Hollywood: A & M Records]).

Have the students tune in.

"This music and slide show has a message for you. Try to let the message sink in deeply as you watch and listen."

The music and slide show is played. The students remain silent for another minute when it is over. The teacher ends the exercise by debriefing.

The Middle Ages Revisited

This exercise requires portable music and a field trip. Take the students into an old church—the older-looking the better. Bring along a recording of Gregorian chant to play, about ten or fifteen minutes in length.

After arriving at the church, let the kids explore for a few minutes in order to get oriented. Then seat them and have them tune in.

"As you listen to this music, look around at the church. Let the music and the sights just flow together into your heart. Let it all sink in. When you feel ready, pray."

The music is played. When it is over, the students remain silent for another minute, and the teacher ends the exercise by debriefing.

A Variation: Instead of taking the students to a church, show them slides of old churches while the music plays.

The Four Seasons

These four exercises are designed to help the students appreciate not only the beauty of creation, but also the majestic rhythm of the seasons. The teacher may select some of the exercises, or use all four. If all four are used, they should be spaced apart so as not to become monotonous and boring to the students. The teacher must obtain slides of nature scenes corresponding to the season or seasons of the year. These are shown to the students accompanied by the appropriate portion of the "Four Seasons" by Vivaldi.

Spring
Have the students tune in.

"Spring is a time of rebirth. All things seem to come alive after the long winter. Everything is young, fresh, new, and clean. It is an exciting time, and it almost looks as though God is creating the world all over again. Watch the slide and music show, and let it sink in."

Springtime slides are shown, accompanied by Vivaldi's "Spring."

"Now take a minute to thank God for bringing the world back to life each spring."

The students remain silent for another minute. The teacher ends the exercise by debriefing.

Summer

Have the students tune in.

"Summer is the green time of year. The trees are full of leaves. Animals that were born in the spring are growing up rapidly. There are long, long days, lazy and hot. Life seems to be just a little slower. Watch the slide and music show, and let it sink in."

Summertime slides are shown, accompanied by Vivaldi's "Summer."

"Now take a minute to thank God for those wonderful, fun, summer days."

The students remain silent for another minute. The teacher ends the exercise by debriefing.

Autumn

Have the students tune in.

"Autumn is a time of the year which is full of changes. The leaves turn from green to golds, yellows, and reds. The days grow shorter and the nights longer. The weather is cooler. Many things begin to die. The animals burrow into the ground to hibernate. The birds fly south. Watch the slide and music show, and let it sink in."

Autumn slides are shown, accompanied by Vivaldi's "Autumn."

"Now take a minute to thank God for the beautiful changes of autumn."

The students remain silent for another minute. The teacher ends the exercise by debriefing.

Winter

Have the students tune in.

"Winter is colder and darker than any other season. Many of the animals are hidden away. Many of the trees and plants look dead, even though they're not. Some people like to say that they are sleeping. When it snows, the world seems like a totally different place. Watch the slide and music show, and let it sink in."

Winter slides are shown, accompanied by Vivaldi's "Winter."

"Now take a minute to thank God for the beautiful season of winter, and all the different things that it brings."

The students remain silent for another minute. The teacher ends the exercise by debriefing.

A Variation: The seasons of the year can be likened to the seasons of a person's life: spring is infancy and childhood, summer is youth, autumn is middle adulthood, and winter is old age. Intersperse the nature scenes with pictures of people at the corresponding stages of life. Invite the students to pray about birth, life, and death.

Thanks, God!

The teacher provides the students with a collection of slides—the broader the range of subject matter, the better. Each student selects a slide that can represent or depict in some way what he or she feels has been God's greatest gift to him or her. When all the students have chosen slides, they are placed in the projector, ready for viewing.

Have the students tune in. As each slide is shown, the student who picked it is to tell what gift from God it signifies. After each student speaks, the teacher invites all to pray in thanksgiving: "Take just a moment to thank God for John's gift." This is followed by a pause of ten or fifteen seconds. If there are more than ten or fifteen students, the prayers of thanksgiving can be done in groups: "Take just a moment to thank God for his gifts to John, Mary, and Jane."

The teacher ends the exercise by debriefing.

A Variation: Instead of having each student speak, simply show the slides while background music is played. "Thanksgiving" music, such as "All Good Gifts" from the musical *Godspell* (New York: Bell Records), would be especially appropriate.

Be Creative!

The following group of meditation experiences is designed to help the kids practice very active and creative forms of prayer. Some of the exercises are even a little off-beat, but that makes them all the more fun. There are many variations suggested for the exercises, and with a little reflection you can think of even more variations to try. There are no limitations; go for it!

Dear God . . .

The students need a pencil and a piece of paper for this exercise. A recording of soft background music is required.

Have the students tune in.

"In a minute you are going to write a letter to God. Take a moment to think about what kind of letter it will be. Will it be a business letter or a personal note? [Pause] Will it be a thank you? An invitation? A request? [Pause] A greeting card? A farewell? A newsletter? [Pause for one minute.] Take your pencil and paper now and write your letter to God. Take your time and make it real."

While the background music is played, the students write their letters. After about ten minutes, or when they seem to be finished, ask them to read their letters over one time. The teacher ends the exercise by debriefing. Students may be encouraged to share their letters, but should not be required to do so.

Variations: Have the kids write about an assigned topic such as a moral issue, a Bible story, a recent event, a person in need, etc. Another variation is to pick a type of letter (invitation, newsletter, etc.) and ask the kids to use that format. Or have the kids imagine that they are a character from the Bible (an apostle, David, Adam or Eve, Mary, Ruth, etc.) and write a letter to God from that character. Or have the kids write telegrams to God, using short, clipped phrasing; let them print out their telegrams on a typewriter or computer printer.

007

For this exercise the students need a pencil and a piece of paper.

Have the students tune in.

"Pretend that you are Agent 007. You have been assigned by God to be here in this world, keeping an eye on things. Your mission is to keep God informed about important things, and to offer him advice about the world. Now it is time to submit a written report to God. Take a moment in silence to think about what you will report. [The students remain silent for one minute.] Now take your paper and pencil and write your report. You have just ten [or five] minutes to get it all down."

The students write for the period of time which the teacher selects. They may work in silence, or with background music. When the time is up, the teacher ends the exercise by debriefing. The students should be encouraged to share their reports with the class.

To God: Personal!

When the disciples asked Jesus, "Lord, teach us to pray," it was not because they didn't know how. Many religious groups within Judaism at the time had special prayers that identified them as members of that particular group. It was something like having a school song. As the disciples began to feel their own specialness as followers of Jesus, they, too, wanted their own special prayer. So we should understand their request to mean, "Lord, teach us our own special prayer."

Often a person today has special things that set him or her apart and which provide a sort of "trademark": a special song, a favorite movie, a certain perfume, etc. It is also nice to have a special prayer.

After these ideas are explained to the students, make sure that each has a pencil and paper, and then ask them to tune in. After they are quiet for a moment, have them write out prayers of their own composition. Tell them that they have about five minutes to accomplish this, but be ready to extend the time if they are still working. While they work, soft background music is played.

At the end of the exercise, the students are asked to pray their special prayers once in silence. The teacher ends the exercise by debriefing.

A Variation: Have the students memorize their special prayers and pray them from memory each day.

Another Variation: Instruct the students to keep their special prayers. To make sure this happens, a storage place in the classroom would be desirable. After a few months, if possible, or at least after a few weeks, have the students spend five minutes of meditation time with their prayers in order to make any changes, additions, or deletions that they think are now appropriate. In the debriefing time, ask these questions:

- How many of you changed your prayer in some way?
- Were you uncomfortable with anything you wrote before?
- Do you disagree with anything you wrote before?
- Since you wrote that prayer, you have grown up some more. Did your growing up change your prayer?
- Are you the same person that you were when you first wrote that prayer?
- Since you wrote that prayer, has your relationship with God changed at all? How? If it has not, how do you feel about still having the same relationship?
- What have you learned about yourself?

Blow Me Away!

This exercise calls upon the students' creativity to help them "get into" an important Gospel story. They need to have paper and pencil on hand.

Have the students tune in.

"Listen to the words of this story. Try to remember every detail."

Mark 4:35–41 (Jesus calms the storm) is read.

"Take your pencil and paper now and rewrite the story as if you were one of the apostles in the boat. Tell what happened and how you felt. Write in as much detail as you can."

The students write for about five minutes while background music is played. Exciting music makes this exercise all the more fun; a good choice is the Second Movement of Beethoven's Symphony No. 9. The students need at least five minutes to do their writing. The teacher should be ready to extend the time period if they are still working. When the students seem to be finished, the teacher ends the exercise by debriefing.

A Variation: This exercise may be extended by having the students share their stories with the group. Comparisons can then be drawn among the various versions.

My Father

For this exercise the students need a pencil and a piece of paper. Have the students tune in.

"Listen to these words. You have heard them so many times. Try to hear them in a new way now. [The teacher says the words of the Our Father, but very slowly and deliberately.] Now, on your papers, rewrite the Our Father, changing the words to make them apply more to you. Use this as a way to speak to God in your own words."

While the students work on this, soft background music is played. After three minutes, or when they seem to be finished, the teacher cuts the music down so that it is barely audible.

"Now take your papers and pray your prayers to God. Make every single word count."

After another minute, the teacher ends the exercise by debriefing.

My Word!

The students need a pencil and a piece of paper for this exercise. Have the students tune in.

"Think of a prayer that you have memorized. [Pause] Now take a minute to pray that prayer in your heart. Make every word count. Really feel when you pray. [Pause for one minute.] On your piece of paper, write down the word or phrase from that prayer that seems most important to you today. [Pause] Now write a note to God and tell him why you chose the word or phrase and why it is important to you."

The students remain silent for another two minutes. The teacher ends the exercise by debriefing.

A Variation: Instead of letting the students choose any prayer, assign one, such as the Our Father. Make sure you pick one that they all know. Several weeks or months after the exercise, repeat it, and ask the students whether they chose the same word or phrase, or a different one. To further enhance this experience, collect the papers the first time, and after the second time, pass the papers back so that the students can make comparisons. This is a good way to help the students to see the richness of certain prayers which we take for granted.

Draw a Prayer

Art is one of the most profound and sincere forms of human communication. Too often in our prayer lives we rely excessively upon words to communicate our thoughts and feelings to God. This exercise is a step in helping the kids to make use of non-verbal prayer. It should be preceded with an explanation and discussion of how art is a form of communication. The teacher should provide examples of art which convey basic messages: sadness, joy, struggle, birth, death, etc.

The students need pencils and paper for this exercise. A recording of soft background music is helpful. Have the students tune in.

"Take your pencil and paper, and draw a prayer. Use your drawing to say something to God. You could tell God how you feel, what has happened to you recently, what you want, what bothers you, or anything else that's on your mind or in your heart. You can make a picture, a diagram, or just lines and curves. The only rule is that you should not write out words."

The background music is played as the students work. After about ten minutes, or when they seem to be finished, the teacher ends the exercise by debriefing. The kids may wish to share their art work and tell something about it. Some however, may feel that it is too private to share.

Variations: Do the same exercise using any artistic medium with which the kids are familiar: painting, charcoal, pastels, sculpting with clay, soap, or wood, etc. There is no reason why the kids should all use the same medium; if the teacher is willing, they may pick from among many. This exercise may be done in reflective quiet with soft background music, or a workshop environment with its attendant work noises and talking may be allowed.

Another variation may be used with kids who are not very artistic. Select any pliable object and have the students manipulate or arrange it to form a prayer. Objects that may be used include: styrofoam cups, pieces of wire, pieces of string, building blocks, a sheet of paper which may be folded and torn, a handful of gravel or beads. The students may manipulate or arrange the objects to say how they are feeling, to ask something of God, to reflect or indicate their present relationship with God, etc.

Art may also be used for group prayer. The entire class can work on a single large collage, mural, frieze, sculpture, etc., to express a prayer of the group. For example, if they have been studying poverty, they could make a collage about poverty which would be their prayer for the poor of the world.

Dance a Prayer

"After the men who were carrying the ark of the covenant had gone six steps, David made them stop while he made a burnt offering of a bull and a fattened calf to Yahweh. Then, wearing only a loincloth, David danced with wild abandon to honor Yahweh. And he and all the Israelites took the ark of the covenant up to Jerusalem with shouts of joy and the blast of trumpets" (2 Sam 6:13–15).

As we can see from the story, dancing as a form of prayer is an ancient practice. It may be exciting for the kids to dance a prayer. (I say *may;* some kids do not like to dance, and would be embarrassed and reluctant to try it, especially in front of other kids.) Explain to the students that they can communicate their thoughts and feelings to God through the motion of their bodies. Those students who wish could then make up their own dance prayers and perform them for the class. The kids should also be encouraged to try this privately at home, where they might be less inhibited.

If you want to try this exercise in class, begin by explaining the concept of dancing a prayer and reading the story about David to the students. Make sure that at least some of them are willing to try it. If they are, have all the students tune in. When all are quiet, invite those who wish to do so to dance their prayers for the class, one at a time. If they need music to be played, that's fine. End the exercise by debriefing.

Producing Prayers and Making Meditations

After the students have been introduced to and practiced a variety of prayer and meditation forms, they should be encouraged and helped to make up their own. Middle school kids love to be creative, and their spiritual thoughts and feelings can be surprisingly profound. The kids may create their own meditation experiences either individually or in teams. It is important to help them focus by suggesting a particular theme or purpose for the meditation exercise. For example, they could be asked to prepare a meditation experience about a problem or cause: world poverty, the nuclear threat, environmental destruction, racism and prejudice, etc. They could prepare an experience which celebrates and gives thanks and praise to God: for a holiday season, an exciting community event, a class achievement, etc.

The kids have to know that they are being taken seriously, and therefore the meditation exercises they create should actually be used for the class. Even if you feel an exercise is poor, it should be tried out; it may surprise you and turn out to be good, and even if it is a failure, that, too, is a learning experience. Be sure to debrief the kids after each exercise, since that is one way that they learn more about prayer and what makes it work.

The kids might also prepare a prayer experience for another class or group of people: a class of younger kids, a parish group or committee, the school faculty, etc.

Exercises for Experts

These exercises have been grouped separately because it may well require special training to employ them successfully. This is true because they tend to elicit from the students strong emotions such as sadness, fear, or a general feeling of anxiety. This is particularly true of "The Good, the Bad, and the Ugly," which has left some students in tears when I have used it. I have included these exercises in this book because they have been some of the most powerful prayer experiences for the kids.

If you feel that you are skilled at group process and particularly if you have counseling expertise, you may wish to make use of some of these experiences. But unless you are confident of your ability to handle whatever strong emotions are dredged up in the kids, stay away from this section!

Death Is Knocking at My Door

Middle school kids are beginning to face their own finitude and mortality in a new way. Most are just beginning to take seriously the idea that one day they will surely die. This exercise helps them to reflect upon evil and death.

Have the students tune in.

"Imagine the most scary and evil thing you can. It might be a monster, or Darth Vader, or something else. [Pause] Many people are afraid of death itself. They want to fight death. The music I'm going to play is about death. It feels scary, and you can hear the fight. Listen to this music with your whole self. Try to hear every note. Try to feel every sound. If you can, become the music so that you and it are the same. It will last about eight minutes."

The first movement of Beethoven's Symphony No. 5 is played with plenty of volume. When the music is over the students remain silent for another minute. The teacher ends the exercise by debriefing.

Global Thermonuclear War

How often we have smiled at President Jimmy Carter's famous gaffe! He reported to America that he had just asked his young daughter, Amy, what concerned her most about the world. She replied, according to Mr. Carter, "Why, Daddy, nuclear proliferation!"

In recent years, many psychologists and professional educators have observed that children *are* anxious about the possibility of nuclear destruction; some of them wonder whether they will survive to adulthood. While some scoff at these observations, I believe that they are true.

This exercise is designed to help the kids to confront their anxieties and to pray about them. It may be preceded with a discussion of the nuclear threat, but does not have to be. It is sufficient to tell them that this song is about nuclear war, and that the bomb is compared to the sun.

Have the students tune in.

"The Sun Is Burning" by Simon and Garfunkel (from the album, *Wednesday Morning, 3 A.M.* [New York: Columbia Records]) is played.

"Take a minute now and tell God how you feel about the song that you just heard."

The students remain silent for another minute. The teacher ends the exercise by debriefing. Plenty of time should be allowed for the students to discuss their feelings about the threat of nuclear war.

A Long Way from Home

Have the students tune in.

"This song is about feeling lonely. While you listen to the song, think of times that you have felt very lonely."

"500 Miles" by Peter, Paul and Mary (from the album, *(Ten) Years Together* [New York: Warner Bros. Records, 1970]) is played.

"Take a minute now to tell God about the times that you have felt very lonely. [Pause for one minute.] Now ask God to be with you always, even when you are lonely."

The students remain silent for another minute. The teacher ends the exercise by debriefing.

Clean Out Your Desk

All of us have certain experiences that "stick" with us for long periods of time: traumatic experiences such as the death of loved ones, a failed test, an accident; happy experiences such as a promotion, a loving relationship, a great vacation. Counselors and other professionals sometimes refer to such events as psychological "baggage"—we carry them around with us wherever we go, and we can be weighed down if we are not careful. This exercise is designed to help the kids find their own "baggage" and to pray about it.

Begin by having the students clean out their school desks. This might take a half hour or so, but let them do it, with all the attendant noise and chaos that will inevitably ensue. After it's all over, have them settle down and tune in for prayer.

"You have just cleaned out your desk. You found some things that needed to be thrown away, and you found some other things that you need to keep. [Pause] Did you find anything that surprised you? Maybe something that you had lost or forgotten about? [Pause] Cleaning out your desk is almost like a treasure hunt. [Pause] Now take a few minutes to clean out yourself. Dig down really deep, all the way to the bottom. See what you find hidden in your mind, your heart, and your soul. Maybe you'll find some things to throw away. Maybe you'll find some surprises. Take a look now. [Pause for three minutes.] Now take a minute to tell God about what you found. If you found anything that hurt, ask God to help you to feel better."

The students remain silent for another minute. The teacher ends the exercise by debriefing, including these questions:

- Did you find any surprises in yourself?
- Did anything hurt? Do you think you need to throw that away? How can you do that?
- Did you find anything that made you happy?
- This could be a regular exercise for a person to do. How often do you think a person should pray this way?
- Would this be a good way for a person to prepare for the sacrament of reconciliation?

A Variation: If it is impossible for the students to clean out their desks (perhaps they don't have personal desks) have them clean out something else personal, such as a locker, wallet, purse, etc. If all else fails, have them clean out their rooms at home as a homework assignment, and do this exercise the next day.

I Confess to Almighty God . . .

Have the students tune in.

"Remember a time when you committed a sin. Pick some time when you did something that was very wrong. [Pause] When did this happen? How old were you? [Pause] Did you do this wrong thing alone, or were other people doing it with you? [Pause] What made you act that way? [Pause] How did you feel when you were doing the wrong thing? How did you feel later? [Pause] Did you get caught by anyone? [Pause] How do you feel now about what you did? [Pause] Take a minute now, and tell God about what you did. God has already forgiven you, because he loves you so much. Thank him for his forgiveness and his love."

The students remain silent for another minute. The teacher ends the exercise by debriefing, but being especially careful to respect the privacy of the students.

A Variation: Have the students examine their consciences by looking back over a certain period of time, for example, a week or a month. This is an excellent way to prepare them for the sacrament of reconciliation, and they should learn this technique well.

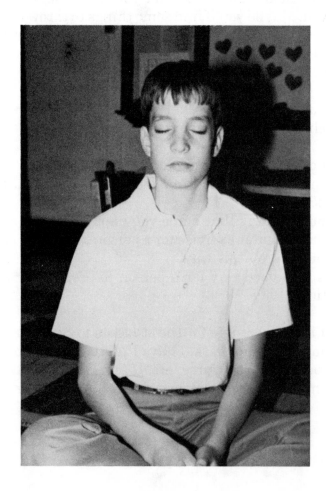

Was I Ever Embarrassed!

Have the students tune in.

"Think back and recall your most embarrassing moment. Pick the most embarrassing thing that ever happened to you in your whole life. [Pause] When did this happen? Who was there? [Pause] Did someone do this to you, or did you do it to yourself? [Pause] Replay the events in your mind as if you were watching it on television. [Pause for one minute.] Take a minute now and tell God how you felt when that happened to you. If it still hurts, ask God to take the hurt away."

The students remain silent for another minute. The teacher ends the exercise by debriefing.

The Good, the Bad, and the Ugly

This exercise should be done *only* when there is plenty of time for debriefing; it might require much more time than usual.

Have the students tune in.

"Pick a happy event in your life and begin to remember it. [Pause] When did it happen? Who were the people involved? [Pause] Where did this take place? [Pause] What did you do? [Pause] Did anyone help you or do anything for you? If someone did, who was it? [Pause] Play the event through your mind as if you are watching it in a movie. [Pause for one minute.] Now speak to God about your happy event."

After a one minute pause, the above instructions are repeated exactly except that the students are asked to remember a *sad* event. After the final one minute pause, the teacher ends the exercise by debriefing.

A Word of Caution: In this exercise, some students will dredge up very painful memories. Some will probably cry. The debriefing becomes very important as they are invited to share what, if anything, they wish. An atmosphere of calm support is necessary. It is likely that some of the students will want to approach the teacher individually after this exercise to tell painful stories. The use of a journal for this purpose would be excellent.

Group Prayer Keeps You Together

There is a difference between praying in groups and group prayer. Praying in groups involves the kind of prayer that people do by themselves; the fact that they are gathered in the same place is simply a matter of convenience or co-incidence. Although they are with other people, their prayer remains essentially individual. Group prayer involves a group of people who, at some level, have formed a community. They gather, and, as a community, they pray.

There are several advantages to group prayer:

- Jesus encouraged group prayer. He said, "Wherever two or more of you are gathered in my name, I am there, too" (Mt 18:20).
- When Christians gather in community to pray, Christ truly is present in a special way, for gathered Christians are his body, the Church.
- Group prayer offers support to each of the members of the group. It helps a person maintain a schedule or regimen of prayer. The presence of others is encouraging. Like jogging, prayer often works better when you have a partner.
- Group prayer allows people to learn from one another. As they pray together, they begin to share their own spiritual journeys, and this helps to teach and encourage other members of the group.

The middle school catechist should encourage the students to become part of prayer groups, or to form their own. If the students with whom the catechist is working have chosen to participate in the prayer times, then it is likely that they will be able to pray as a group. If, on the other hand, they are a class group, their feelings of trust and their desire to pray as a group may not be sufficient to allow group prayer.

The exercises in this book may be used either for prayer with groups, or for group prayer. If they are used for group prayer, I suggest the following general format:

- Have the students tune in.
- Do the meditation exercise with the students.

- Invite the students to pray aloud, spontaneously, one at a time. This should never be forced. All of the kids should know that at these times for spontaneous prayer, they are free to speak up or to be silent and pray along with those who do pray aloud. In their spontaneous prayers, the students may be reacting to the experience of the exercise. For example, after *Hawaiian Punch* in the Introduction, a student might pray aloud, "Father, thank you for giving us wonderful things to eat." If after sixty to ninety seconds none of the students have offered prayer, the catechist should simply move on to the next step.
- Invite the students to pray the Our Father together, in these or similar words, "Let's finish our prayer by praying together in the words that Jesus taught us." If the students feel comfortable with it, joining hands for the Our Father is most desirable.
- Always conclude group prayer by debriefing.

Instead of spontaneous prayer, the group may try a litany style prayer modeled after the prayer of the faithful at Mass. In this case, students offer a petition, concluding "We pray to the Lord . . ." and all respond. The response may be the traditional, "Lord, hear our prayer," or any other suitable response which is pre-arranged with the group.

When a religious education class can achieve group prayer on a regular basis, their spiritual formation will make great progress. Group prayer is a very faithful experience and will help all of the participants become stronger Christians.

Journal Keeping Helps You Pray

Keeping a prayer journal helps people grow spiritually by providing a means to reflect upon their prayer. It helps them to see cycles in their prayer lives, to find the prayer forms which are most appropriate and effective for them, and to note progress that they make over longer periods of time. Many spiritual directors feel that keeping a prayer journal is absolutely essential for spiritual growth.

Keeping a prayer journal as a daily or weekly exercise can be helpful to middle school kids as well. All of the advantages are there, but it is difficult for a middle school student to sustain journal keeping efforts for a very long time. The teacher can help youngsters establish and maintain journal keeping by teaching them how to do it and by continuing to encourage them in their efforts.

It helps a youngster to have a good quality book or binder for the prayer journal; this makes it seem more special, valuable, and worthwhile. A three ring binder with pockets in it seems to work best for middle school kids: it allows them to add or delete material easily, and the pockets may be used to hold handouts or other class materials which are relevant.

Here are several ways to use a prayer journal with your class of middle school kids. It is best to use several different methods of journal keeping, since the kids will quickly become bored with the same method.

- Writing notes in the journal can become part of the regular debriefing routine after class meditation exercises. The kids can note their initial reactions to the experience before any discussion, and then can share what they have written. After discussion, or during it, they might find other thoughts to record. The questions suggested in the Introduction for debriefing are all relevant for prayer journals.
- Many of the exercises suggested in this book involve having the kids write out something. This material can be placed in the journals and kept.

- The prayer journal is a good place to write notes to God. These can be long, reflective letters, or simple little notes dashed off in a hurry. These notes become written prayers, and can be referred to later.
- Journals can help the kids to set their prayer "agenda." During the day, as they think of things they would like to pray about, they can jot these down in the journal. Later, when there is more time for prayer, they will have a reminder.
- Prayer journals are good places to write daily or weekly reports. Here the students can write about not only what is going on in their lives, but how their prayer has been for the day or week.
- The teacher can produce and give to the students "Prayer Report Forms" like the one below. These can be filled out by the students after class prayer exercises as part of debriefing, or taken home to be used on a more individual basis. It is not necessary for the students always to answer every question.

PRAYER REPORT FORM

Today's Date _____ Time of Day _____

Describe briefly the prayer experience you just had. What happened, and what were you thinking or praying about?

Rate your prayer experience on the scale below.

5	4	3	2	1
excellent	very good	good	fair	poor

What reasons do you have for selecting the rating you did? In other words, what made this prayer experience good or bad for you?

What did you learn about yourself from this experience?

What did you learn about God from this experience?

Other comments or reflections:

The kids should know that their journals are their own; they are private property. They should be taught that what they write in their journals is considered and assumed to be private. The teacher should respect this privacy, and the students should respect the privacy of each other. Students may be invited often to share what they write in their journals with the teacher or with the entire class, but such sharing must always be voluntary. The students should know that they may choose to share only part of what they have written, or none of it at all.

The teacher should be flexible about letting the kids use their journals in ways they find helpful. For example, some students may just "doodle" in their journals; this doesn't hurt anything, and it might help them to think and pray. Let them do it!

The teacher might set up regular meetings with the students to discuss their progress in prayer. At these times, it would be helpful for the students to share their journal material with the teacher. As long as the youngster's privacy is respected, this kind of sharing can be most rewarding for both student and teacher. It is an opportunity to teach the kids on an individual basis, to encourage them, and to share in their lives and struggles.

To keep prayer journals, middle school kids need lots of help, encouragement, and reinforcement. If journal keeping can become an established habit in the classroom setting, it has a chance of continuing over into the kids' daily lives outside of the classroom.

Debriefing:
The Essential Ending

Debriefing is an essential ending for every prayer and meditation exercise described in this book. To debrief, or not to debrief: that is *not* a question! You simply have to do it. So, what is debriefing?

Debriefing is *sharing*. The kids have just had an experience, and it is time for them to share what happened. Their experience may have seemed significant and important to them; it may not have. But the opportunity to speak about that is always significant and important.

Debriefing is *getting support*. The prayer experience may have left a student with a negative feeling, such as boredom, frustration, anger, fear, anxiety, sadness, etc. If he or she can talk about this, the teacher and students are able to

offer support: to say that having such feelings is all right; to respond sympathetically and to offer advice; perhaps to share the same feeling. Often a student will be left with a very good feeling after an exercise. He or she might feel happy, content, at peace, close to God, etc. In sharing this, the student can be encouraged to continue working at prayer; the good experience can be affirmed by others as good and worthwhile.

Debriefing is *reflecting*. Often after a prayer experience, we just aren't sure what we felt, what happened, or whether it was good or bad. We may feel some confusion. It helps to reflect, or "bounce" ideas off of other people. By talking to others about our experiences, we can clarify our thoughts and feelings.

Finally, debriefing is *testing*. By asking the students to evaluate the prayer experience, the catechist can test it: not only to see if the exercise itself was helpful, but to see if the catechist presented it well. Sometimes during debriefing the catechist may receive certain helpful comments: the volume of the music was too high or low; there was a disturbing background noise; part of the exercise seemed silly to the kids, etc. Debriefing can also help the kids to test their own experience of prayer. It helps them to discover and define the types of prayer that are most helpful or appropriate for them. It helps them to work on little practical problems, such as maintaining correct posture or breathing. It is a chance for them to ask themselves and to be asked whether they are really putting enough energy and care into their attempts at prayer.

Debriefing is a form of *group process,* to use some current jargon. Helping the students to debrief means helping a group of people communicate with one another. If you often get only grunts or awkward silence from a group when you try to help them have a discussion, try following these simple rules for group process:

- Ask them questions that are open-ended, and which cannot be answered by a yes or a no. If you ask a yes or no question, the answer you can expect will have only two or three letters! Here are some sample questions that I often use in debriefing after a prayer experience:

  - How was that?
  - Can you say more about your reaction to the exercise?
  - What feelings did you have? Do you still have them?
  - What did you learn about yourself?
  - What did you learn about God?
  - Would you like to pray that way more? How can you do that?
  - If you didn't like the exercise, why not?
  - Is this type of prayer right for you? Why do you think it is or isn't?
  - Was that a prayerful experience for you? Why, or why not?

- Can you suggest any changes in that exercise that would make it better?
- What are things that help you pray?
- What are things that block your prayer, that keep you from praying like you want to?
- Do you think God spoke to you? What did he say?
- Were you listening to God?

- Make sure that the kids respond to questions one at a time. It is very important for them to listen to each other. Listening to each other is how support and reflection can take place.

- Any sincere thought or opinion is all right and the teacher should receive it positively. Perhaps a student disliked an exercise and was bored; it is important that he or she feel free to say so. Encouraging honesty is the only way for the students and catechist to test the experience. If students learn that they can be honest with the teacher in little things, they will feel that they can also be honest about big things.

- The students must never be forced or coerced into making comments during debriefing. An atmosphere of freedom must prevail. Sometimes during prayer very personal and private things happen in a person's heart; that privacy should always be respected. Let the students contribute to the discussion whatever they can give freely and willingly.

- After you ask an open-ended question, give the kids time to think and respond. It sometimes helps to repeat the question two or three times, with ten or fifteen seconds of silence in between each time. Don't be afraid of silence; often it is a sign that during prayer, something good happened. Be quiet long enough for the kids to give a response.

- Concentrate on the feelings and emotions that the kids had during the experience. Steering the discussion into this area helps to deepen the content. It touches on ideas and themes that are the most important to the kids.

- Often a student will share with the group something very important. This is a gift which he or she has given to the group. The teacher should thank the student for sharing.

- Be a model for the kids. Show them the kind of sharing that you think is appropriate. Offer your own comments about the prayer experience, e.g., "I was feeling very close to God because . . ." Show them how to be clear, and how to be kind and respectful toward others.

To sum all of this up, here are the ABC's of debriefing:

Always debrief after every prayer experience.
Begin by asking, "How was that?"
Concentrate on feelings.
Draw out responses by asking open-ended questions.
Everyone has a right to speak or not to speak.
Finish by summing up and offering any advice you have.
Go for it!

Trouble Shooting

As you work with middle school school kids, teaching them about prayer and leading them in meditation exercises, they will, from time to time, have negative feelings about prayer, or problems with it. And because they are middle school kids, they will tell you about their complaints loudly and clearly! Here are some of the more common complaints, and constructive responses which can be helpful.

"My back hurts!"
Kids often cannot tell the difference between a straight back and a stiffly arched back (see "Finding the Right Channel: Tuning In" in the section "How To Get Started"). When backs are stiffly arched, they hurt. Work with the kids to show them how to keep their backs straight, but relaxed. It may help to lean back against a wall, but only if the spinal column is kept vertical; that means you must sit right up against the wall. Demonstrate this for the kids and help them relax while sitting upright.

"I get dizzy when I do this!"
The dizziness is probably caused by hyperventilation, or breathing too much air too fast. Have the kids slow down their breathing to the point that they are breathing as slowly as possible. It should take several seconds to inhale and exhale.

"My mind wanders. I can't pay attention to this. I daydream."
Remind the kids to focus their attention on their breathing and the flow of air in and out. It is natural for the mind to wander, particularly if a person is anxious about anything. Tell the kids that each time they find they have lost their concentration, they should simply focus once more on the flow of air.

You can help train the kids to concentrate by starting with rather short periods, say twenty or thirty seconds, and then gradually building up. Be sure to tell them not to be discouraged and give up. If they find they have begun daydreaming near the beginning of an exercise, rather than quitting, they should simply

126

return their attention to their breathing. Try these two imperatives: be soft and gentle, but be persistent.

If several kids in the group are having trouble concentrating, perhaps the timing is wrong. You might be asking them to meditate too close to the beginning or ending of the class period, or when distractions such as background noises are more pronounced than normally.

"I get sleepy when I try to meditate."

This will happen quickly if the kids do not sit upright when they meditate. Remember, tuning in has a tranquilizing effect on the person. Sitting upright in the manner described is important because it combines relaxation with *alertness*. If the kids try to meditate at bedtime, and if they do so lying down, they are almost sure to fall asleep. Of course, there is also the possibility that a student is simply not getting enough sleep at night.

"I'm trying to pray, but I've got nothing to say."

This is not a problem! Remember, prayer concerns our relationship with God, and relationships go in both directions: there is a time to speak, and a time to listen. Having nothing to say presents a person with the wonderful opportunity to be quiet and listen for a change!

Sometimes when a person has nothing to pray about, it is a good time to do spiritual reading or obtain some other input, such as listening to sacred music. This is also a good time to make use of memorized prayers. The reason we have memorized prayers and prayer books (and even the Liturgy of the Hours, a vast and complex literature of daily prayer) is that we cannot always think of everything that needs to be said.

A person should not feel guilty or deficient when he or she has nothing to say to God. St. Paul must have been thinking about this when he wrote: "In the same way the Spirit also comes to help us, weak as we are. For we do not know how we ought to pray; the Spirit himself pleads with God for us in groans that words cannot express. And God, who sees into our hearts, knows what the thought of the Spirit is, because the Spirit pleads with God on behalf of his people and in accordance with his will" (Rom 8:26–27).

"I'm listening, but no one's talking."

This is a problem! At least, it can be. When you feel that God is not speaking, the first question to ask is: Am I *listening*? Sometimes we fill our prayer time with so much noise and input, and so many of our own words, that we are simply unable to listen.

But even when Christians are quiet, there are times when what they feel most deeply is God's absence. This is a normal experience in a person's spiritual life, and usually goes in some kind of cycles. Many of the great saints had terrible struggles with this feeling of God's absence; some of them called it the desert experience; St. John of the Cross called it the "dark night of the soul."

The desert experience is a reminder that prayer is a gift from God. Sometimes he will be present to us in a way we feel, and sometimes not. We may not understand the desert experience or why it happens, but we can be confident that it will change. One day God will lead us out of the desert, often when we least expect it, and in very powerful ways. So when the kids come with this complaint, tell them to "hang in there," and things will change.

"I can't find any time to pray."
This is a common problem. You need to pick a definite time of day for prayer, e.g., upon rising, bedtime, after dinner, etc. Praying while taking a bath or shower works especially well for some people. Another time to consider is a boring time each day, such as time spent riding the bus to school or work. Finally, arriving for Mass early provides a nice period of time in a nice setting for prayer.

Many people who cannot find the time for prayer are looking for too much. They get excited about prayer and decide to spend thirty minutes or an hour each day at it. After a few days, they discover that this amount of time is unrealistic for them, and instead of reducing it, they get discouraged and quit praying altogether. In short, over-ambition can be a stumbling block.

Middle school kids should begin slowly, planning to spend just a minute or two once or twice a day, at definite times, in prayer. After this little pattern is well established, they can gradually build up that prayer time, making it longer and longer, until they find what is right for them. Each individual will need to find his or her own rhythm.

Sometimes it helps to plan regular prayer times with a group or with the family. The expectations and support of others can help a person to be more consistent with time spent on prayer. It's a lot like jogging: you usually do better if you find a partner.

"I keep forgetting to pray."
The answers to *"I can't find any time to pray"* apply here as well. In addition, the students may need some kind of reminder to help them remember to pray. Often a strategically placed symbol will do the trick. An old Catholic favorite is to put a cross on the pillow when making the bed; at bedtime, seeing the cross

reminds a person to pray. Other similar symbols might help: an appropriate picture placed on a person's desk; a Bible on the bedside table.

"I'm bored!"

This is another common problem with middle school kids. First, the teacher needs to make sure that the kids have been taught tuning in properly; without this preparation, few of the meditation exercises described in this book will hold the kids' attention.

The teacher should make sure that a great variety of prayer forms and techniques is used. For example, doing Scripture meditations every day for a week will be too monotonous, and the kids will become bored.

Sensory stimulation in prayer helps to combat boredom. Many meditations make use of music, symbols, pictures, writing materials, etc. When the kids complain of boredom, give them some stimulation.

Finally, prayer can become especially boring for kids if it is too passive. Middle school kids love activity, and they want to be in the very center of the fracas. Take advantage of that natural inclination and make them work as they pray. There are plenty of meditation exercises in this book which demand a lot from the kids, such as writing, feeling, imagining, etc. Keep the activity level high.

"I hate this! Meditation stinks!"

When you first hear this, check out the response to *"I'm bored!"* Remember, too, that middle school kids learn best in an atmosphere of mild coercion. Those who loudly voice their hatred of an activity sometimes need just a little bit of gentle persuasion. But when the teacher has to resort to punishment to make the kids cooperate with meditation, it is usually harmful and counter-productive.

The resistant child can sometimes be helped by tapping in to his own creativity. If the teacher can steer such a child into the direction of creative activity with meditation (see the section "Be Creative"), he or she might become interested.

But there is no assurance here. Sometimes you will run into a child who simply will not find anything good about prayer and meditation. If that happens, be willing to let it go: the types of meditation exercises presented in this book are not for everybody. The teacher should not feel responsible for the spiritual lives of the kids. Even though they are still children, this is something they have to choose for themselves. Remember the old adage about leading the horse to water.

Finally, do not try to make a child feel guilty because he or she does not like meditation. Comments such as "Good students cooperate and enjoy this" or

"What do you think Jesus would say about this?" or "It's a sin not to pray" simply do not help. Furthermore, they are not fair comments to make.

"When I meditate I get scared. Meditation upsets me."
All of us can become upset from time to time when we pray, particularly when our prayer focuses on traumatic events in our lives. But when a child frequently becomes anxious while meditating, it is usually a sign of some emotional disturbance or problem. The anxiety is already there in the child, and the quietness of meditation allows it to bubble up to the surface. If you work with a student who frequently becomes upset while meditating, you should consider referring him or her for counseling. Persons who are experienced at this, such as guidance counselors, priests, and principals, may be of help to you. The child's anxiety is a warning signal, and could indicate a serious problem. Make sure you aid the student in finding the proper kind of help.